Legacy of an Immigrant Farmer

By: Mary Luchsinger Sperling

- Follow your dreams with a vision -

Mary Luchsinger Sperling

- Dedicated to my father, Henry Luchsinger Sr. -

Family Tree

MATERNAL GREAT-GRANDPARENTS

Onondaga, New York

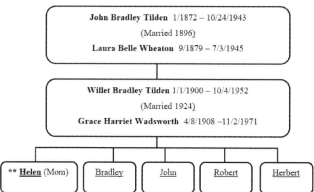

PATERNAL GRANDPARENTS

Schwanden, Switzerland

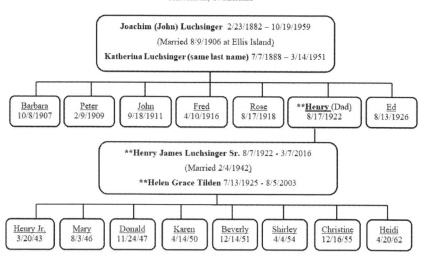

Acknowledgments

I am grateful for life on the farm and the hundreds of experiences that were shared with my seven siblings; Hank, Mort, Karen, Beverly, Shirley, Christine, and Heidi and the many tough lessons of life taught by our parents. Blessings to my oldest brother, Hank, for enduring the many challenges, along with my dad, to keep the family farm alive.

I thank my friends, Bonnie Bronson, Marisue Smith, and to members of the Holiday Park 3W's group in Lakeland, Florida for their ongoing encouragement, praise, and support. Thank you to Doreen Sullivan for the feedback from her review of the draft. My son, Steve for his extraordinary technical knowledge and assistance in getting the book published, I thank you.

Most of all, I want to thank my wonderful husband of nearly fifty years, Clifford for his love, input, and patience. Much thanks to our sons Dan, Steve, Matt, and Tim who inspired me to share my vision of my story and the excitement of our precious grandchildren who have waited patiently for the finished book.

Table of Contents

Chapter   Page

Chapter	Title	Page
1	Schwanden	1
2	Traveling to America	7
3	New Home in Upstate NY	14
4	Newly Married	22
5	Fulfilling the Dream	29
6	Farm Children	37
7	New Beginning	49
8	Working at Forward Farm	54
9	Willowbrook Farm	57
10	The Old Farm Reborn	69
11	Free Labor, Not Free	75
12	Chickens	78
13	Making Maple Syrup	83
14	Berries and Cherries	87
15	Unwanted Critters	93
16	The Bull	96
17	Summer Sundays	99
18	Annual Vacations	109
19	Discipline	114
20	Birthday Barter	121
21	Playtime and Pets	124
22	Expectations	134
23	Mom's New Jobs	141
24	Doctor Visits	149
25	Treating Sick Cows and Calves	157
26	Hunting	162
27	Social Calendar	168
28	Christmas	176
29	Dad's Endless Jobs	189
30	The Blizzard of '66	186
31	Keeping the Farm	190
32	Mary Goes To Work	195
33	Weddings	205

Chapter	**Page**
34 For the Love of Farming	211
35 Coping with Loss	218
36 Jamie	227
37 Hard Days	236
38 Change	241
39 One Final Thought	249

Family Recipes	**Page**
Grandma Tilden's Chocolate Cookies	253
German Green Beans	254
Boiled Raisin Cookies	255
Barbecued Chicken Sauce	256
Mom's Date Nut Cake	257
Fried Squash	258
Vanilla Cream Graham Cracker Pie	259
Hamburg Gravy	261
Swiss Steak	262
Oyster Stew	264
Apple Cake with Vanilla Sauce	265
Best Lemon Meringue Pie	267
Sloppy Joe	268

A Final Note From the Author 269

Chapter 1

Schwanden

My grandfather, Joachim Luchsinger sat alone on top of Mettmenalp. Tears filled his eyes as he thought about his lonely life on top of this vast mountain. His mother, Anna Barbara Zwifel had died a long time ago – in 1885 when Grandpa was three. Now suffering the loss of his father, Johann Peter, a short three months ago, he felt like a misplaced orphan. The death of both parents added the pressures and obligations of taking care of his stepmother and family of fourteen children. At sixteen all his formal schooling was put aside and Grandpa was forced to seek out full-time work to help support his many siblings.

Joachim yearned to be down in the valley with his friends and family in the tiny Swiss village of Schwanden, a municipality of the Canton Glarus. The German-speaking inhabitants numbered a mere 2,400 hardworking farmers, cabinetmakers, carpenters, textile workers, and lumberjacks. From afar he could faintly make out the neat brown chalet homes lining the main road, with flower boxes of red geraniums dressing every window. Colorful hollyhocks and edelweiss were meticulously planted against the walls and fences of the Swiss cottages and barnyards. Along with gorgeous flowers, neatly arranged vegetable gardens covered the front lawns of each Swiss home.

Vegetable garden in front of a Swiss Home

From Grandpa's view on top of Mettmenalp, he could distinguish some homes and barns that were precisely built into the sides of the mountains. (Such homes were more resistant to avalanches and the earth served as insulation in summer and winter.) The clanging of cowbells could be heard in the distance as the cattle chewed their cud. The Linth and Sernf rivers met in Schwanden, just fifty miles from Zurich, and one main road connected it to other small villages. The much needed newly-installed electric Swiss railway from Weesen transported Swiss to other parts of Switzerland

Schwanden

and Europe. Klaussenpass, the only road to the high alpine over to Altdorf, stayed open from June through September.

"Oh, to be with people! I don't want to be high in the Alps fourteen hours every day, every single day, alone," Joachim whispered under his breath. There was nothing for Joachim to do during those long, lonely days but think and dream; the herd took care of itself most of the time. Lying in the rich meadow grass and gazing at white puffy clouds floating along in the blue sky made a setting perfect for dreaming. Grandpa felt the strong urge and vision to do something besides the isolated chores of herding goats, sheep and cattle. But he had no choice: Grandpa had to help support his family of many half sisters and half brothers after his dad remarried and then died.

At sixteen, herding goats and cows was the only thing my grandfather knew. Daily he gathered the herd of animals from nearby farms and guided them up the steep, sloping mountain terrain to Mettmen. His day started before sunrise at four o'clock with the tiring physical exertion of a two-hour journey up the meandering mountain trail. Ruts and jagged rocks covered the rugged makeshift route. With a walking stick in hand, Grandpa carried a carefully wrapped hunk of good cow cheese and half-loaf of day-old bread, and maybe a few sugar cookies. If he was lucky, some birnbrot, dough with dried pear filling, would be in his leather satchel formerly used for school books. At the end of his meal he carefully shook out the cheese and crumbs from the cloth wrapper and folded it to be used again and again in days to come. Grandpa also carried a canteen strapped over his shoulder filled with water from home, and throughout the day refilled the canteen from the lake at Garichtisee. Slithering on his belly over to the edge of the shallow lake, he carefully filled his canteen with refreshing, ice-cold mountain water.

Lake Garichtisee

Grandpa kept watch over the herd of twenty to thirty goats and cows during the long summer days on top of Mettmenalp. An array of colorful blooming blue alpine cornflowers and vibrant wildflowers, plush green meadow grass, and crisp clear lake surrounded him. Mettmen grasslands gave the herd nourishment while dreaming nourished Grandpa during those long days. At four p.m. Grandpa filled his canteen with cold mountain water once again, collected his herd and started back down the curving and twisting mountain road, kicking up stones and sometimes booting the same rock until it disappeared over the mountain edge. He completed this journey seven days a week for a few Swiss francs until the weather changed in early fall. Farmers kept their livestock in barns in the lowland throughout the late fall, winter and early spring months. Then when ice and snow left Schwanden and lush grass started growing again, Grandpa would start the ritual of daily mountain trips to the top of Mettmenalp.

As soon as his herding job came to an end in late September, Grandpa worked in the mountain woods surrounding Schwanden. With the use of workhorses and bobsleds, the dangerous and physically challenging job of cutting and hoisting the heavy logs onto sleds taught him the principles of hard work. From the age of sixteen, he repeated this tiring chore, day in and day out. He never complained but always yearned for something different, but he had no choice. Dreaming in the meadows and lying in bed at night, his thoughts focused on anticipation, and he waited for an opportunity for change.

During the winter of 1900, Grandpa was asked by a neighbor, Gabriel Schneider, if he would be interested in traveling to America. Gabriel's brother, Casper was in America and wanted a motivated, hardworking young man to work on his farm. In those days the chance to leave Schwanden and go to the "Land of Opportunity" was not just challenging but exciting. Grandpa had been given the chance to chase his dream.

But he had no extra money, he could not speak any English, and the only work experience he had was cutting timber and herding domestic animals. He also had to think about leaving his family and friends. Grandpa labored for days over this decision.

*Klausenpass to Atdorf
Road closed during the Winter*

The trip to America cost thirty-five dollars, plus he needed spending money for living expenses. Grandpa only had twenty dollars saved from his jobs; however, it was customary for the village to collect money to help aspiring Swiss go to America. With the family's and neighbors' meager contributions, enough money was accumulated to send Grandpa Luchsinger on his way. An old life was ending. A new life was beginning!

Schwanden

Chapter 2

Traveling to America

A few days after his 18th birthday, Grandpa said his heartfelt goodbyes to his family and friends in the only place he knew as home for the promise of a better life. The tearful departure was filled with well-wishers and advice. His family told him to be aware of people trying to take advantage of him, cheat him, give him bad advice, or steer him in the wrong direction.

His brother Peter advised Joachim to carefully save his earned money when he arrived in the new country. "Just in case you don't like America, you can return to Switzerland," Peter said. Being a young foreigner and not knowing the English language could be troublesome, Peter thought to himself. "Remember, you will be an American. Learn the English language!" Peter yelled out as Grandpa boarded the train. Joachim looked back, taking one last glimpse of his brother, possibly for the very last time. Even though some immigrants came to America to escape religious persecution or political cruelty, Grandpa sought a chance to reach out and grab opportunity and seek out the American dream he had heard so much about.

Swiss Farmland in Schwanden

Grandpa Luchsinger, and his neighbors Sebastian and Emanuel Schmidt (brothers), and Gabriel Streiff left Schwanden by train for Le Havre, France, their departure point, just before the sailing date of March 1, 1900, for the long journey to America. There was much comfort and relief in knowing other Swiss immigrants were also making the journey, all speaking the same Swiss-German dialect.

Grandpa purchased a steerage ticket for thirty dollars and had only a few dollars left. Lucky for Grandpa, he did not need a passport from Switzerland – passport laws were not enforced until late 1900, a few months after he left Europe. The timing for Grandpa's departure was planned perfectly, with no waiting around for the next sailing to add to the cost of lodging in a nearby immigrant hotel.

Brief preliminary procedures, including thirty-one simple

questions, were recorded on the manifest lists before boarding the ship by a German-speaking agent.

"Do you have at least twenty-five dollars, Joachim Luchsinger?" the agent asked routinely. Knowing he had less, Joachim nevertheless replied, "Yes!" Nothing was going to stop Grandpa from getting on that ship. Without hesitation, the officer allowed him to pass through to the next stage of the processing. Joachim heaved a sigh of relief.

Each passenger in the steerage compartment of the ship had to have a medical physical, and a brief exam was performed looking for medical ailments obvious to the physician. Each passenger and his baggage had to be disinfected. Vaccinations were performed to prevent diseases from spreading on the ship, and after new immigrants landed on American soil. The ship's owners paid for the process, a welcome relief to Grandpa's wallet.

After passing all the requirements, Grandpa and countless other immigrants from numerous countries were herded down a steep, narrow staircase to lower decks with sparse windows. Each passenger was assigned a numbered berth containing a burlap mattress stuffed with hay, and a life preserver, which duplicated as a pillow. The berths were stacked two-high with another set of berths side by side. A tin pail, cup, and utensils were given to each passenger for meals. After rinsing the dishes off after each meal, Grandpa placed them at his berth under his makeshift pillow for safekeeping. The meager food cost forty cents a day for some passengers but was included in his passage fee. There was no choice given, but usually porridge (hot cereal), salt pork, pea soup, coarse bread, and bland stew were available. The food scarcely filled his belly. Everyone's nerves were on edge. There they ate, slept, and passed the days playing cards or talking with other passengers who spoke the same language.

The two-week journey across the Atlantic Ocean became harder as conditions became more unpleasant with each passing day. Due to unsanitary personal hygiene and lack of proper ventilation, foul body odor penetrated the stale air of the crowded quarters. Some immigrants became sick; others short-fused. This caused hostile skirmishes, but scuffles were quickly broken up. Seasick passengers were everywhere. Continuous rough motions and movements of every passing wave made life unbearable. Fear of icebergs, cold March days, and long, lonely nights in darkened quarters added to the misery of the long journey across the Atlantic Ocean.

The steerage compartment located at the bottom of the ship also played havoc with passengers' emotions and feelings. Grandpa felt confined like a prisoner in his windowless hole. He was used to fresh mountain air and open spaces, but steerage passengers were not allowed on the upper decks. Sometimes he would spend hours talking with Emanuel and Sebastian Schmidt. Grandpa endured the dreadful conditions, but waited with an open-mind for the next phase of his journey. He had already learned patience and perseverance at an early age.

On March 13, 1900 Grandpa's ship docked at Hoboken, New Jersey, but his grueling journey was not over. As a safety measure, the ship was quarantined when it landed, customary for all incoming ships filled with immigrants. Immigration inspectors boarded the ship. First and second-class passengers and U.S. citizens were quickly processed and allowed to leave the ship as they were not required to be examined. Steerage passengers had more difficult red tape.

Fortunately, the ship arrived before five p.m.; ships arriving later than five would anchor in the Lower Bay of New York Harbor until the next morning, and that meant another dreadful night on the ship. After arriving, every passenger was directed to a waiting area to be processed. Grandpa was given landing and medical inspection cards and again examined for any contagious diseases or illnesses, as were all other steerage passengers. Doctors would check for rashes, looking carefully at hands, neck, and face. His exam took no more than two or three minutes, and he wore a tag with his name and manifest number clearly written so it could be easily read by the inspectors. Every immigrant had a manifest number written on a name tag large enough to be seen from a distance. Inspectors often knew six or more foreign languages, helping the process along.

The ship sailed slowly north to the Narrows, entering Upper New York Bay and then into Manhattan where it docked. The newly-erected Statue of Liberty was in clear view as the ship passed.

Grandpa could hear cheering passengers exclaim with delight as they sailed past this famous landmark.

After the initial processing of each passenger, immigrants were directed onto barges in groups of thirty according to their individual manifest numbers. Personal baggage was placed in piles on the lower decks. The barges went to Ellis Island.

The next leg of Grandpa's journey was being ushered along with other immigrants up steep, wide stairs to the Registry Room. Unknown to immigrants, moving to the next area of inspection meant facing another test to see if they qualified to stay in America. In an area located at the top of stairs, inspectors looked carefully at each new immigrant's gait, ability to climb the stairs without shortness of breath, or other signs of disability. For Grandpa, physically challenging work cutting timber and herding goats in the high Alps conditioned him well to pass with flying colors.

Immigrants needing further examinations were marked with a red X or some other special coding on their coat. Some quick-thinking immigrants facing deportation would turn their top coat inside out to avoid being sent back to their native land. Others who had a detected illness or disability were immediately deported. Laws were strict. Any immigrant who was too ill or feeble-minded to have a job and support himself or his family was forced to leave America on the next ship, back to the port they left.

Grandpa's final test consisted of a two-minute interview from a German-speaking inspector to verify that the thirty-one questions asked in France matched the information on his manifest. Except for the few passengers who exhibited medical or mental problems and were deemed disabled, all other immigrants were cleared to enter onto American soil.

    Joachim was allowed to pick up his meager belongings. A German-speaking agent directed him to the Money Exchange to trade his Swiss francs for the daily American currency. He said goodbye to his Swiss friends, who were staying in the New York City area to visit relatives before heading to Syracuse. Departing words in German-Swiss were shared by all: "Take care, be safe, great prosperity until we see you again."

    Grandpa took his meager money and headed to the railroad ticket office for a one-way ticket to Syracuse, New York. He was sent to a waiting area marked for the New York Central railroad line in the ferry terminal. When it was near time for his train to depart Manhattan, he was directed to the train terminal.

    Sadly, he would miss the Schwanden friends who gave him comfort and reassurance. Now Joachim Luchsinger was totally alone, surrounded by thousands of strangers – even more alone than on his mountain top.

Chapter 3

New Home in Upstate New York

While waiting at the train station anticipation and excitement grew. Joachim Luchsinger's last leg of the exhausting two-week voyage from Schwanden, Switzerland to America had become a reality. Grandpa was given a box lunch and his exchange of money safely secured in his pocket, all $1.35, when the conductor shouted, "All aboard!" With prompt responses from the waiting passengers, they swiftly moved to doors of the New York Central Railroad train. Grandpa did not understand what the conductor yelled, but by his tone of voice knew it meant "get on the train" – and he promptly followed everyone else's lead. Along with carrying his satchel, Grandpa held his ticket, money, and meager belongings firmly to his body.

"America is great, but among the good are thieves, homeless, and crooks seeking to take advantage of immigrants who appeared lost or need a friend. Don't trust anyone," he remembered. Fatigue and exhaustion filled Joachim's body. Lack of sleep and worrying about the future entangled his soul. "No turning back now," he thought to himself.

The train ride to upstate New York turned out to be uneventful, however, the March coldness seeped throughout the train. Grandpa's thin body was chilled to the bone. His only winter coat was wrapped tightly around him to prevent the brisk bitter cold air from entering his space. Most of his head was covered with the wool hat with attached earmuffs that he wore in the Swiss Alps cutting timber. While nibbling on his box lunch given to him at the train station, Joachim sat back observing from the train windows, the lush surroundings of wilderness with splendid pleasure. Spectacular snow-covered mountains, the Mohawk River flowing freely with a hint of ice along the banks, clusters of bare forests, and small farms with open fields and stone fences encrusted with snow were visible, much like his homeland in Switzerland. Several stops along the way including Albany and Utica made for a long journey. Homesickness started to set in. "Why did I leave Schwanden? I don't know one person. I am terrified of what I have gotten into." Grandpa quietly muttered to himself.

Ten hours after leaving New York City, the conductor yelled, "Syracuse, Syracuse!"

Immediately Grandpa stood up, collected his small satchel containing his life's belongings and followed other passengers to the exit door. Scary thoughts filled his head. How could an eighteen-year-old Swiss boy have the courage to make such a mission? Grandpa was alone in a big city, speaking only a dialect of German and worrying about his transportation to Onondaga Hill, where he would be working for a stranger, in a strange country, on a farm he knew nothing about. Taking a deep breath, he reassured himself that life is an adventure and the only thing to fear is fear itself.

Franklin and West Fayette Streets were in the heart of the city. The weather was bone-chilling, much like Schwanden a few weeks before. Snow was in the air and the piercing arctic wind created a great deal of discomfort. From a distance Grandpa could hear someone yell "John!" and then again, "John!" The man looked directly at him, and Grandpa remembered that his name, Joachim in Swiss, was John in English. This would be his new American name. All legal papers, employment, and signatures for anything would now be signed John Luchsinger.

The fellow approaching Grandpa spoke in German and said he was Casper Schneider. "My new boss speaks German," thought John with a sigh of relief.

More confident now that he would be able to communicate with people, but he remembered what his brother had advised about being an American and the need to speak English.

They walked over to the hitched-up team of horses and swiftly climbed onto the buckboard. Casper and John had over an hour's ride to their home on Bussey Road, and left the train station heading southwest toward Onondaga Hill. Snow covered the ground and the blustery snow blistered Grandpa's face. Traveling up the steep, winding road from the valley made for a brave quest. Grandpa hung onto the sides of the carriage seat. He could not

New Home in Upstate New York

believe Syracuse had so many hills and wintry cold.

When the buckboard turned left off West Seneca Turnpike onto Bussey Road, mounds of snow banks and snow-covered fields and forests were on each side of the rough road. Just up one more hill, passing the Ollie Isabelle farm house on the right, Grandpa saw on the left of the road, a yellow farmhouse and two yellow barns nearby. At that moment, he did not know he would be traveling Bussey Road hundreds and hundreds of times in the days and years ahead. Years later Grandpa said, "I had a pocket full of dreams, burning ambition, and somehow a feeling that I would find in America the things that I had heard about, but never dreamed I would be the owner of this very farm."

Grandpa met Casper's wife Maria Bertha Luchsinger Schneider and their five daughters ages three to twelve. The Schneider family and Grandpa visited while enjoying warm potato and ham soup made with a rich buttery milk, fresh crusty bread, and hot frothy coffee – half strong hot coffee and half milk, like Swiss drink. A feeling of security and comfort filled Grandpa's lonely heart. Casper, speaking in German-Swiss, shared stories with him about the history of the farm and his own aspirations and dreams. Casper did not own the farm; he rented from Grant Rowland. He also wanted a piece of America and planned to buy a farm someday with every penny he could save.

The girls slept upstairs in the two-story farmhouse. Katherine, the youngest of the five siblings had a twin sister,

Margaret, who was stillborn. While Bertha was pregnant, a stone was kicked up from the horse-drawn plow and struck her. The baby was buried in the front yard. Grandpa was aware of the raw pain in their voices, still pulling at their heartstrings.

Stories were shared about the Schneiders coming over fifteen years earlier from Schwanden and Elm, a small village of four hundred residents south of Schwanden where the highway ends and surrounded by three mountains. They started their own family in America, making Grandpa even more determined to make this place his new home. Hearing laughter from the girls rallied Grandpa, helping him get over being homesick and feeling lost in a foreign country.

Grandpa was given a tour of the house and was directed to his bedroom, located just off the dining room. He could see his breath and feel the cold chill as he entered the room. Snow was on windowsills, and a small bed and heavy handmade covers were neatly folded at the end of the bed. His belongings hardly filled one drawer of a large walnut dresser.

Grandpa was taken to the barns housing the livestock. He had no work experience with milking cows or growing crops, and therefore would be working his first month for room and board only. He was not afraid of hard work, but ambitious and motivated, eager to learn farming skills. Throughout the spring, summer, and fall when the farm demanded much more laborious duties, Grandpa was paid nine dollars a month – not a lot of money working from early morning to late evening, seven days a week.

After the crops were harvested, Grandpa would again work for his room and board only. Grandpa's boss Casper and his wife spoke a Swiss dialect of German so Grandpa had no chance to learn the English that he knew was important to be successful in America. So, taking a risk Grandpa left the Schneider farm and went to Marcellus about ten miles away. He worked for Frank Seeley throughout the winter at the handsome amount of nine dollars a month plus room and board. There he learned additional farming techniques and skills, but, more important he had the opportunity to learn English. Frank Seeley's elderly mother, a retired school teacher, lived with the Seeley family and taught him English during long winter evenings.

As spring approached, a salary of twenty dollars a month was offered to Grandpa. Without hesitation, he stayed and learned English, banking his monthly wage in hopes of fulfilling his dream of success and happiness in America. Over the next two years his salary increased to twenty-five dollars and his reputation for being a responsible, hard worker spread through the farming community. As any farmer would agree, a good hired hand is difficult to find, a great commodity, and when you do find him, he should be treated fairly.

After two years working at the Seeley farm, Grandpa accepted a position at the Hazard Estate in Solvay, NY to care for their superior Brown Swiss cattle. Grandpa took advantage of learning more farm skills and the ability to show prize cattle. Every opportunity to learn and improve supported his belief that some day he would own his own farm in this great land called America. He continued to expand on his knowledge of English, learning new farming techniques, and saving his money, every penny he could, for his dreams.

In 1905 Grandpa wrote to his oldest brother Peter, a letter carrier, asking him if he knew a Swiss girl who would be willing to come to America and be his wife. At almost the same time, Katherina Luchsinger asked the mail carrier if there was a letter from someone wanting a wife to come to America. Katherina was born on July 7, 1888, and knew my grandfather from school, but she was five years younger. John and Katherina started corresponding, and Grandpa's letters described the beauty and opportunities offered in America. Because they both had the same last name before they were married, they traced their ancestry in Switzerland to see if they were related. The Swiss kept a pedigree of everyone in Switzerland, and my grandparents were able to trace back to the 1600's without finding that they were blood-related.

In the spring of 1906, Grandpa Luchsinger sent Grandma Katherina the money required to come to America. With great strength and courage, eighteen-year-old Katherina accomplished all preliminary requirements, obtained a Swiss passport, and collected her personal belongings, left her family and friends and traveled by ship to meet a man she barely knew in a foreign country. She unknowingly experienced the same thoughts: fear of the unknown, and the challenge of forming a new vision of happiness, seeking love in a strange country, so far away from her family. Her new husband had experienced the same thoughts six years before in 1900.

By late July 1906, just after her eighteenth birthday, Katherina left Schwanden for France by train along with a friend, Gabriel Scheiff and his wife. Gabriel had a job waiting for him at the Nottingham farm through connections made by Grandpa. Katherina welcomed Gabriel's help and companionship and they boarded the ship that would take them to America.

On August 4, 1906, Grandpa headed to Ellis Island in New York City by train to meet Katherina, his soon-to-be wife, but, the ship was two days late. When the vessel finally docked Grandpa received permission to visit her on the ship and planned to bring her to Syracuse. Because the United States government had just passed a law stating "if a girl came to the United States alone she could not go ashore to stay here unless she had relatives in the USA or was married. There was nothing else to do but get married."

Grandpa rushed around looking for a Lutheran minister to marry them. They were married on August 6, 1906, in New York City. According to Grandpa in a newspaper interview with the *Syracuse Post Standard* in 1941, they were the first couple to be married after the new law went into effect. Now two lives were joined in a new country to pursue their dreams.

New Home in Upstate New York

Chapter 4

Newly Married

August 1906

After completing strict immigration procedures, John and his new bride purchased her ticket for the journey back to Syracuse. The lengthy experience was much easier than six years before when Grandpa couldn't understand English. He could now communicate with the German and English-speaking agents, and guided his wife through the terminal to where they waited patiently for the departure to Syracuse.

Warm August days and cool evenings were a beautiful time to travel to upstate New York by railway. Traveling in August, the trip was much more pleasurable than in the bitter cold of March, as John had done six years before. The same route – using the New York Central Railroad to central New York – through mountains, lush green fields in the valleys, rich fertile farmland, past rivers and lakes brought back anxious memories of such a brief time ago. John was proud of his accomplishments with the English language and gladly helped Katherina with the new language since their Swiss-German dialect was her only language.

When Grandpa and Grandma Luchsinger arrived in Syracuse they had about three hundred and fifty dollars left after buying furniture. They continued to work at the Hazard Estate, with Grandma doing household chores, planting, hand-weeding, and harvesting garden produce to be sold at the Syracuse market and for their personal use – much like she had done in her native Schwanden village.

Their first child, Barbara Margaret, was born on October 8,

Newly Married

1907, just a little over a year after they were married. Grandma continued with vegetable gardening, household chores, and the demanding job of taking care of Barbara. Grandma took Barbara with her to the garden and entertained her while she planted, weeded, and harvested vegetables for the market.

Grandpa yearned to develop an understanding of how to care for, and show prize Brown Swiss cattle. This knowledge was essential to be successful. He learned about the importance of combining hay, grain, and corn silage in just the right ratio to produce milk for man – a little ahead of what farming is about today.

Grandpa took every opportunity to work on his English, mindful of the importance of connecting and interacting with other local businessmen and farmers and understand American laws. English was a necessity to be a successful farmer and blend into the community, and as years went on and my grandparents had their own children, English was the first language at home, even though they were fluent in Swiss-German. On rare occasions German was spoken at home. According to my dad, those were the times when my grandparents didn't want their children to know what they were talking about, similar to parents spelling out words to other adults when subjects are not intended for young ears.

During the second year of their marriage, John and Katherina were eager to start out on their own; however, they didn't have enough money for a place and livestock. Instead they rented a farm owned by Sidney Lewis near Drumlins, now the Tecumseh Golf

Newly Married

Club just outside of Syracuse. The fifty acres were on shares. Lewis provided some cows and Grandpa was able to buy one, a few tools and team of workhorses. In addition to milking cows, my grandparents raised chickens, and planted and harvested a variety of garden produce which they sold at the farmer's market on North Salina Street, working side by side.

Their second child, John Peter, called Peter, was born on February 18, 1909. Grandma diligently continued the many household and garden chores in addition to nurturing two small children. She worked hard occupying her days with endless hours of laundry, cooking, keeping house along with the essential field work.

The next year, Grandpa and Grandma Luchsinger worked one hundred-fifty acres and one hundred seventy-five acres the following year, using their team of horses for tilling and harvesting. John hired farmhands. However, problems erupted as most of the help was short-lived. Once the hired help received their pay, they headed to Syracuse just a few miles away and never returned. Consequently, Grandpa had to do most of the farming himself.

Eventually Grandpa's health began to suffer and he was told by his doctor to stop working so hard. He was completely exhausted from working seven days a week, long hours of hard labor. Grandpa John took the doctor's advice, and in August 1909 sold his share of the crops and livestock for one thousand dollars and took a short rest. Eager to work, he accepted a position through an acquaintance, as manager, at the Worthington Jersey Ranch in Marion, West

Newly Married

Virginia. The work was much easier, but Grandpa still had an overpowering vision of being part of the American dream and owning his own farm.

A third child, John Jacob was born on September 18, 1911 in Marion. Grandpa managed the herd of cattle, willing to learn new methods in farming while Grandma tended to her three young children. She worked in their garden and took care of all the household responsibilities.

My grandparents were thrifty and saved and saved, and after three years at the Jersey Ranch they took a brief trip back to central New York to visit friends in Onondaga Hill. During the visit Grandpa heard that the very first farm where he had worked, Casper Schneider's farm, was for sale for three thousand dollars. Casper, who had rented the Bussey Road farm, purchased a seventy-acre farm from Court Rich on Cole Road.

Without hesitation Grandpa bought the fifty-two acre farm. He put one thousand dollars down and a neighbor who believed in him loaned him the two thousand dollars and held the mortgage. Lacking money to buy the necessary farm equipment and livestock, though, Grandpa and his family of five went back to the West Virginia Jersey Ranch to earn and save enough to buy the needed equipment and livestock to start farming on their own.

For two more years Grandpa rented out the farm in Syracuse while earning money, saving every extra penny earned on the West Virginia ranch. In 1914, fourteen years after leaving Switzerland as

Newly Married

a young, penniless immigrant, my grandfather and his family arrived in Syracuse to their American dream farm on Bussey Road. Grandpa named his new farm, Silver Springs Farm. (He saw the spring water on the hillside reflecting in the sunlight and it reminded him of silver.) After purchasing tools, and chickens, and three purebred Jersey cows at the cost of five hundred dollars, Grandpa had five dollars left in the bank. (He never touched that money. He said the money was for a rainy day, and it was still in the bank when he died in 1959.)

John and Katherina worked as a solid team in every aspect of their life together. No county, state or federal agency helped out the needy, hungry, or destitute at that time. Neighbors helped neighbors, and relatives helped family – that was the norm. When my grandparents had difficult times or when money was tight, they sold chickens or eggs to pay a bill or buy groceries. But they found happiness and wealth in the American dream, and were motivated through difficult times, combating obstacles, never giving up, and continuing every day with a strong desire to prosper.

Grandpa's experience and skills obtained working on the Hazard Farm, and as manager in West Virginia, taught him with proper fertilizing and cultivating, how to develop rich farmland. He learned the importance of tending his crops and livestock with care. Grandpa emphasized improving butterfat from his Jersey cows, and worked diligently, selectively breeding cows to develop a higher percentage of butterfat. He got rid of undesirable cows that did not

Newly Married

perform up to his expectations, and soon his herd was nationally known. As time passed Grandpa purchased more farmland until he had one hundred sixty-two acres of rich fertile soil.

Grandpa and Grandma's family expanded with the birth of four more children. On April 10, 1916, Fridolin Franz, another boy was born, known as Fred by his family and friends. Another baby came on August 17, 1918, named Rosa Maria, and called Rosie by many. My dad, Henry James, was born August 7, 1922, and their seventh, Edward Harry, born August 13, 1926. There were five boys and two girls: Barbara, John, Peter, Fred, Rosie, Hank and Ed.

Values and a strong work ethic were instilled in each of their children. Each child was required to do chores and had daily responsibilities before and after school. My dad was the sixth child born on the farm, and from the time he could barely walk he had chores to do. But school was a large part of their lives. My dad told me once, "You walked the mile and a half to school each day, paid attention, and even did homework at night after doing evening chores." My grandfather and my father both believed learning was important, but also assumed if you could do hard manual labor you could earn a living to provide for your family. Dad said many times, "If you are willing to work, you can make money to survive." Dad was not afraid to work or generously help a neighbor, farmer, family member or friend, valuable lessons learned from his father. These principles and hard work were beginning to form a new life, and it would be a good one.

Newly Married

Chapter 5

Fulfilling the Dream

Many years passed. Grandpa and Grandma persevered in their belief and vision that America was a land of opportunity and continued following the American dream.

Grandpa developed a herd of superior purebred Jersey cows using skills learned working for other farmers in his early years in America. He traveled throughout the United States and abroad, selling and buying the finest quality stock. The family also showed livestock at fairs throughout the Northeast. My dad, Hank remembered going to Harrisburg, Pennsylvania, and Columbus, Ohio, with his father before interstate highways, hiring a driver and cattle truck to transport their prize Jersey cows for shows. Grandpa and Grandma were excellent business people, using these shows to meet and make sales with some of the best herdsmen. Besides speaking their native language, by now they could speak fluent English, which they knew to be very important.

They visited Switzerland in 1938, the first time since leaving in 1900 and 1906 respectively. Europe was in the middle of war and crisis. Their Swiss families in Schwanden were troubled and anxious about the conflicts of their European neighbors even though Switzerland was impartial. America remained free of turmoil and unrest. Grandpa and Grandma were glad to visit but happy to return to America.

Exhibiting cattle, raising seven hardworking children, and developing a successful family farm brought pleasure and happiness to my grandparents' life. Attending fairs was a family event. They showed at the Eastern States Exposition and National Dairy Shows, and the children growing up received their first showmanship lessons at 4-H shows at the county fairs and the New York State Fair. Grandpa strove for perfection in everything!

On some occasions, my grandparents would exhibit in Springfield, Massachusetts before the NYS Thruway and Massachusetts Pike were developed. Instead of transporting by truck, reservations were made at the railway station located at Geddes and Erie Boulevard. Grandpa and his family would load the cattle on railroad cars customized for hauling cattle safely. Some of the family would drive, meet their show cows at the destination station, and then make arrangements for delivery to the fairgrounds; some family members stayed at home to feed and milk the herd. Many smaller county fairs at such places as Whitney Point in Cortland County, Auburn, Watertown, and Batavia were attended by Luchsingers with their prize herd. (I will never forget in 1957 – at the age of eleven, while showing at the Parish Show near Auburn, Grandpa personally gave me a good piece of advice I will never

Fulfilling the Dream

forget. "Always look at your animal you are showing or the judge, not at the people in the audience," Grandpa yelled sternly. He exuded authority and respect. Scared to death by his firm comment, I did exactly what he told me to do – you by no means disobeyed him!)

My grandparents and their children participated yearly at the New York State Fair held in late August and early September in Syracuse, just a twenty-minute drive from home. Some family members stayed all night sleeping in the cattle barn, while others traveled back and forth daily transporting a large cooler packed with sandwiches, fruit and goodies for the day workers and overnighters. Purchasing food at the fair was saved for a special occasion or treat; too expensive for their modest means. Every day the stake-rack truck was loaded with hay and straw from the farm used for feed and bedding for their show cows. Sometimes extra feed was sold to herdsmen that traveled great distances to participate at the fair.

Grandpa was so determined to show his prized herd at the Fair, one year when the cattle truck was not working the family spent an entire day walking the herd the ten miles through the countryside over to Solvay. The family had to work together as they were familiar with moving cattle between fields, but steering the cattle over such a long distance was a new and difficult challenge. This amateur cattle drive was only successful through determination and old fashioned grit.

1940 – Grandma Luchsinger

As a result of the Luchsingers' hard work, many awards and honors, including Premier Breeder (inscribed on a purple banner), the highest award at the State Fair, and other recognition was regularly received. Grandpa was very proud of these accomplishments. For many years the family won ribbons and money at the fairs, but what was even more important, estate owners visiting the fairs inspected Grandpa's herd of Jerseys, and often paid top dollar for any Jerseys he was willing to sell. Grandpa's Jerseys produced quality milk with a high butterfat content that not only helped with his own income, but attracted the attention of wealthy farmers throughout the United States and beyond. He took care of the little things – properly caring for his animals and treating them gently. "You treat your animals like ladies," he often said.

Fulfilling the Dream

1939 – Hank showing cattle at the New York State Fair

Showing cattle at the New York State Fair has been a family tradition since 1921. Year after year, the Luchsingers loaded up their prize cattle and headed over to Solvay with their precious cargo. The only period they did not show was during World War II when the fairgrounds were used as a military base for field artillery. Grandpa's son Fred purchased the Silver Springs Farm in 1950, but Grandpa continued to work the farm until his death in 1959. Uncle Fred continued operating the Silver Springs Farm with the help of his children. His son Chuck bought the farm in 1986. After taking ownership he modernized the farm upgrading to bigger tractors and

Fulfilling the Dream

an improved milking system. Chuck and his family continue to participate at the New York State Fair, showing their fine Jersey herd, and still receive many special awards, including Premier Breeder which has been won for decades.

Fall of 1941 – Silver Springs Farm
From Left: Fred, Grandpa, Grandma, Hank, Ed and Rossie

John Luchsinger, a penniless immigrant from Switzerland had become a successful dairy farmer, herdsman, and nationally-known breeder of Jerseys. He dreamed on top of Mettmenalp as a young boy of doing something challenging with his life, took a risk coming to America. In March, 1942, the national magazine Successful Farming ran a front-cover picture of the Luchsingers' success story. When the magazine's representative visited the fall before, my dad Hank, his brothers Ed, and Fred, and sister Rose, all living at home, were included in the article. (The bombing of Pearl Harbor – December 7, 1941, occurred between the magazine's

Fulfilling the Dream

interview on the farm and publishing of the article.)

Grandpa developed creative ways to make a successful living, working seven days a week, twelve to fourteen hours a day, to accomplish this. He took pride in his home: surrounded by colorful flowers including hollyhocks which reminded him of his Swiss homeland. He balanced his life with work, play, and rest having regular routines and eating hardy, healthy meals. He recycled before that word was introduced into modern society, and he taught his family to waste nothing. Grandpa made a relentless effort to overcome obstacles, taking risks and never giving up. He learned the benefits of making good soil even better, fixed things that were broken, made do with what he had, obeyed the laws of the land, saved his money for that rainy day, and was a good neighbor and friend.

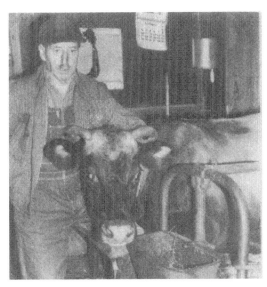

Grandpa Luchsinger

A hundred years after John Luchsinger's arrival we are faced with tremendous changes in our heritage, customs, and values. Grandpa was grateful and appreciative for the opportunity to be in America. He did not take handouts; there were none. When entering the United States in March, 1900, laws were enforced that refused the unfit, or jobless. Grandpa had a job as a farmhand and had the insight and determination to learn English and the wisdom to use it. He focused on fulfilling the American dream he had heard so much about. Now his children would share in that dream.

1937 – Luchsinger Family Portrait
Back Row: Rose, Fred, Pete, John, Barbara
Front Row: Ed, John, Katherina, Henry

Fulfilling the Dream

Chapter 6

Farm Children

Priceless lessons were instilled in my dad, Henry, and each one of his six siblings. At an early age, everyone was taught to work as a team, sharing the workload and cooperating. Whining, complaining, or moaning were not tolerated. Each season of the year Grandpa had dictated responsibilities for the children. Fall, winter, and early spring, there was a mile and half walk to West Seneca Turnpike to the one-room schoolhouse each day. Boys were required to bring in firewood and start the wood-burning stove, bring a bucket of water from the well, and shovel a path to the door on snowy days. Children were segregated according to grade, the youngest being in front and the oldest in the back of the room. The teacher directed individual lessons to each grade while the other students had specific assignments to do. Students would overhear the previous lessons year after year, often reinforcing what was taught. It was most embarrassing for an older student to not know an answer, and a younger snot-nosed second grader to have the answer. This gave students the incentive to study and know their material.

No horseplay or fooling around was allowed in Mary Strife

Emmert's class. She was a large, hefty woman who demanded an orderly classroom. If there was any possibility she might tell my grandparents of negative behavior or disrespect, the children knew there would be all hell to pay. Mrs. Emmert's daughter Doris was Dad's age and she sat in front of him in the classroom. The Schwartz brothers, farmers down the turnpike, also attended the one-room schoolhouse.

Dad and his siblings each had a defined chore or two before going to school. Some helped with milking while others fed the young stock or chickens. One job my dad Hank had daily was grinding mangles. Mangles, or sugar beets, were harvested in late September and covered with leaves or straw. When the cold weather settled in they were placed in the cellar of the homestead. Before school each day, Dad had to go to the root cellar, a large room with a dirt floor under the house, and carry up a heavy bushel basket of mangles, the size of cantaloupes, and take them to the barn to grind for the cows. Mangles were sweet and improved butterfat content of milk. The key to raising Jersey cows was the butterfat count. Cows loved the beets – much like us enjoying dessert.

Grandpa was always getting teased about his small Jersey cows. Other farmers would joke about them being, "No bigger than a goat." Grandpa would laugh and respond with, "Yeah, but I get a bigger paycheck." Even at that time, creameries would measure the butterfat content of the milk and base the pay on amount of butterfat in the milk. When combined with the smaller Jersey cow eating less food they were a higher profit cow.

*1941 – Harvesting Sugar Beets (Mangle)
From Left: Grandpa, Hank, and Fred*

My dad hated grinding mangles. One morning before school, he was mindlessly cranking the machine and nearly lost a finger in the grinder. Grandpa taught him the correct way of holding the mangle and where to place his fingers, but Dad was in a hurry. He ended up with a chewed-up middle finger. Dad wrapped the blood-soaked finger with a clean piece of cloth, the finger still bleeding, and then he went off to school, suffering with pain all day. He saw no doctor, no emergency room visit or urgent care medic to stitch his finger or clean the wound. He didn't take a day off from school or his responsibilities at home – he had to tough it out. The lesson learned was to be careful of sharp objects, they cut! Focus on your job, never be in a hurry, and respect equipment and machinery,

Grandpa preached that day (and many times in the future) to his children. Our dad respected equipment and sternly lectured us years later about the importance of being aware of danger around farm equipment and farm animals.

Dad's school days were repetitive. He knew precisely what to do. When my father came home from school he immediately changed his school clothes, hung them up for the next day, and put on his work duds. He did this every day. Everyone wore two changes of clothing each day, one for work or play and one for school and clothes were washed once a week. Then there might be cookies or bread and jam for a snack to hold the kids over until dinner. Hand-cranking the corn sheller was one of Dad's jobs after school at a young age. He had to feed the livestock, and when he got older, share in daily chores of hand-milking the cows. Mowing the lawn with a hand mower using kid power was a regular chore for one of the children. After the yard was mowed, handheld pruning shears were used to carefully trim shrubs and bushes. Grandpa enjoyed the green grass and an array of colorful flowers surrounding his home. The boys also had to stack firewood outside the kitchen and daily fill the wood box in the kitchen for the cooking stove, never missing this chore. If you did, you were in big trouble!

After chores and dinner Dad completed his schoolwork and was soon in bed. Morning came quickly. The same routine took place each day, but Saturdays the children had more complicated chores, such as cleaning out stalls or moving hay – if the family was not at the Regional Market selling farm produce. Sometimes the family would attend the Lutheran Church in Syracuse where my grandparents were members. Sunday afternoons were a time of rest and social gatherings.

Food at the farm was plain and simple but plentiful. Five hard-working farm boys and two girls had enormous appetites. Dad was taught to appreciate everything served at mealtime. One of his favorites was head cheese, meat from the jawbone of the pig. The family also ate trite, (the first or second stomach of a cow used for food) liver, heart and kidneys. Chuckling to himself, Dad once said, "Mom used to boil the piss out of the kidneys!"

Grandma Luchsinger cooking on wood stove

Farm Children

Grandma cooked foods grown and raised on the farm. Every Sunday night cornmeal mush was served and Monday morning Grandma would cut the mush into squares and warm the leftovers in her cast iron skillet. Occasionally she would fry the mush in butter with some eggs. During the short blackberry season, in the coolness of the evening, the family would go along the hedgerows and pick plump, dark blackberries. A couple of pies were made, and the remainder of the berries canned for winter months.

My grandparents would buy fifty-pound bags of cornmeal in cloth bags with calico patterns, and then reuse the freshly-washed bags for pillowcases, aprons, and skirts. Small leftover pieces would be neatly packed away to be used for winter projects of quilts or lap blankets. Everything was recycled or salvaged in some way.

Fattened pigs were slaughtered in the cool fall before snow fell. A raging fire would be made under a large cast iron kettle, filled with water, outside in the barnyard near a large sturdy tree. After the water came to a rolling boil, a tripod would be centered over the kettle. The butchered pig would be hoisted up by a chain attached to the tree, looping the chain through its feet. The pig was then dipped quickly into the scalding water several times. Using a handheld scraper, the small coarse hair was scraped off the pig. This procedure was used to avoid seeing or eating any hair in the pork skins, especially the backside of slab bacon.

Smoking the pork was done once the wood-burning furnace started in early fall. My grandparents didn't have a smokehouse so improvised using their chimney. Family members climbed to the roof with feedbags filled with large pieces of pork. Securely attaching a wire to these hunks of pork, they slowly lowered them down the chimney until they met a wire grate. After many days of smoking pork, the meat was cured and used as ham and bacon. Grandma Luchsinger, with the help of her sons, then placed the meat in the cool cellar for use all winter.

Salt pork was a necessity. Slabs of thinly sliced fat would be placed in layers in a wooden barrel, sprinkled with salt and then the process repeated until all the pork fat was used up. The barrel was then placed in the cool, dark root cellar. When needed, Grandma would fry up the pork the same way we fry bacon, and serve it with homemade flap jacks or, as dad would say, "panny cakes." Salt pork added flavor to any kind of beans (especially kidney beans) grown on the farm, and stretched potato dishes for their hungry family.

Besides pork, my grandparents sacrificed a cow for eating each year. When freezing weather arrived in cold, snowy central New York, a cow would be selected and killed for feeding the family. Grandma canned beef and pork. Dad told me, licking his lips, "The beef and pork were delicious, tender and flavorsome."

The rich, fertile soil on Grandpa's farm was perfect for growing vegetables. Planting a massive garden of corn, beans, Swiss chard, beets, cauliflower, peas, carrots, tomatoes, cabbage, navy beans, and a variety of squash were treated as staples at mealtime. Each year Grandma processed hundreds of jars of vegetables and fruits for the long winter months, storing them neatly on crudely made shelving in the root cellar. The overflow was stored in her pantry located off the kitchen. The quart and half-gallon canning jars were washed carefully and reused year after year – she never bothered with pint jars with her large family except for jam.

Fortunately, besides growing their own vegetables, Grandpa and Grandma took advantage of the Saturday market for extra income during the growing season. Every Friday night the whole family gathered flawless vegetables, examining each carefully, and stored them in the cool cellar in wooden bushel baskets until early the next morning.

Market mornings, Grandma Luchsinger prepared a quick breakfast of oatmeal and bread, and packed lunches for later in mid-morning. By five a.m. everyone swiftly loaded the back of the model T Ford truck. Some of the kids climbed in the back of the open truck with their wares and headed to North Salina and Pearl Streets in Syracuse, where a paid-up rented stall was waiting. Dad and his younger brother Ed, and sister Rosie usually went to the market with Grandpa and Grandma. Older members of the family stayed behind to do the milking and morning chores, weeding or harvesting. At the market, eggs and garden produce were carefully placed on a makeshift table or were displayed proudly in bushel baskets for the public to admire. Sometimes the family would take a few live chickens or rabbits to sell. Grandpa made sure the quality was good, requiring perfection in everything that met the public's eye, a lesson he learned as a boy in Switzerland and taught his own children.

After the Saturday market closed, any items not sold would be loaded back onto the truck and taken back to the farm to be used in meals for the next few days. Nothing ever went to waste.

The family looked forward to stopping at Columbus Bakery on the way home for warm delicious Italian bread. Store-bought bread was a treat. Grandpa Luchsinger would buy ten loaves of hot, deformed bread (or "crooked bread" as Dad called it,) for a nickel a loaf. Crooked bread tasted no different than regular bread. The kids in the back of the pickup would pass a loaf around, yanking off pieces, eating the whole loaf before arriving back home on Bussey Road.

The work was not done, though. They needed to unload the truck one final time, taking the unsold vegetables either to the kitchen or cellar. Then there was a late lunch, – Dad called it a dinner – a quick nap, and chores in the barn. Dinner was always at noon and their largest meal. Supper was usually some kind of leftovers except when the kids were in school. (In Switzerland, the tradition of a big meal at noon and light supper is still being observed, in addition to an hour of rest. Most stores and businesses still shut down from 12:00 to 2:00 p.m. in Schwanden today.)

Besides storing food in the cellar, barrels of alcohol were found in farm family cellars. Most farmers had a barrel or several barrels of specialty beverages. From the farm orchards, ripe pears, plums, and grapes created almost pure alcohol for delicious wine shared at celebrations with neighbors, friends and family. Hard cider made from orchard apples was a staple in almost every farmer's cellar and my grandfather's farm was no exception.

  Christmas was celebrated as a special day at my Grandparents' farm. A real hemlock was cut down in the woods and placed in the cool parlor. Twenty-four real candles would be lit for a brief time each day for a few days. A few ornaments were distributed on the tree and a star placed on top. The tree also had some bubble lights that intrigued the younger children and grandchildren. The tree would stay in the cold parlor (along with some beef since there was no refrigeration) during the winter months. Once it was so cold the goldfish bowl filled with water froze along with the fish; when the ice thawed, the fish survived! My father's Christmas gifts consisted of pants, socks, and maybe a shirt. Dinner was beef or chicken, usually chicken. Wild turkey roamed around the farm, but they never ate one. Dad said wild turkeys are usually tough.

  The boys slept upstairs in bone-chilling bedrooms most winter nights. Piles and piles of comforters and quilts kept them warm. The pee pot would freeze over most nights during the winter. The girls slept downstairs in one of two bedrooms. They slept in the same small room Grandpa Luchsinger slept in as a hired hand the first year he came to America working for the Schneiders.

Before Grandma Luchsinger died in 1951, at the age of 63 of breast cancer, married family members visited the farm most Sunday afternoons. Christmas Day was special and each grandchild received a nice gift from a cousin who secretly had his or her name. (At the age of five or six I was thrilled to receive a red book bag that buckled in the front from Sally Luchsinger at the Christmas party.)

Family gatherings on Sunday would be a brief two hours. Some would bring homemade cakes and Grandma always had breads, particularly Swiss birnbrot, sweet bread with a filling made of dried pears. Delicious homemade pies or cookies were made ahead and stored on the pantry shelf located off the kitchen. Ice cream and good hot perked coffee or rich Jersey milk were available for the twenty or thirty family members. The brief two-hour social gathering for siblings connected each with stories of their weekly trials and tribulations and successes. Grandpa and Grandma offered advice and expressed their thoughts – they never hesitated to give advice, good or bad. Once they told Mom and Dad if they didn't stop buying cars they would never have any money, not a comment my parents wanted to hear! My grandparents had endured life's experiences and only wanted the best for their seven children. The children took their wisdom in stride, choosing what to attend to and what to dismiss.

1948 – A Sunday gathering at the family homestead on Bussey Road Dad holding Mary, Mom holding Don, Hank Jr. sitting on grass

By three or four o'clock, family members would head home to their own farms and chores feeling refreshed from the afternoon visit. Another week of twelve to fourteen-hour days of hard work was facing them all.

Sadly, after Grandma Luchsinger, the matriarch of the Luchsinger family died, family members still visited, but the family did not celebrate their connection on Sunday and Christmas as they once did. But the old traditions were not forgotten, and soon would be incorporated into new families including my dad's.

Chapter 7

New Beginning

On the corner of Norton and Young Roads, just two miles from my dad's Bussey Road farm, my mother, Helen Tilden, lived with her parents and four younger brothers. She attended grade school in the one-room schoolhouse at the corner of Abbey and Norton Roads, the same school her mother Grace Wadsworth had attended years before. Mom made the daily walk a few hundred yards down the steep hill from her home, passing her grandparents' (John and Laura Belle Tilden) farm.

Helen and my dad Hank were dating during the fall of 1941. She saw my dad several years earlier while taking final exams in the gym at Onondaga Central High School. But Dad dropped out of school at sixteen to work on the farm full-time, as did all his brothers – a typical practice of farm boys in the 1920's and 30's.

Mom started her senior year of high school just after turning sixteen. Doing well academically, Mom skipped fifth grade, a common practice years ago if one qualified. She continued to be an excellent student at Onondaga Central, a new centralized school formed after the Works Progress Administration (WPA) built large centralized schools during the depression years under President Franklin Roosevelt's New Deal.

*1935 – Schoolhouse on Norton Rd (Sunday School Class)
Front Row: (left to right) in sled John Tilden, Rev. Baker as Santa
Second Row: Helen Tilden Luchsinger (Mom), unknown, Leona Rouse, unknown, John Wadsworth Jr., Jim Wadsworth, Bruce Norton, Carl Schmidt, Brad Tilden, Arthur Wadsworth, Paul Schmidt, Hilda Schmidt
Back Row: Dorthy Schmidt, Edith Kelsey, Gladys Schmidt, Jane Wadsworth, Mabel Schmidt, Grace Tilden (Grandma)*

Mom was eager about starting her senior year, with dreams of becoming a teacher after high school. Seniors had privileges to work in the lunchroom scraping china dishes and stacking them for other students to wash. The wages, a few cents each day, gave Mom spending money and lunch.

But all was not well. Within weeks of the opening of school, she began to feel nauseous and extremely tired. Sickened with the thought and aroma of food in the mornings, she played with her oatmeal until it was time for the school bus. She avoided eating, telling her mother she was just nervous and excited. Each day Mom faced the challenge of working in the cafeteria around food and as weeks passed, and the queasiness and churning in her abdomen continued, she knew something was wrong.

The Tilden family doctor, Dr. Gak, had his practice a few houses from the new first through twelfth grade school in South Onondaga. One day Mom secretly gathered up the courage to walk the quiet street to his office to have him verify that she might be pregnant. He confirmed her suspicions. Fearing that her parents would disown her and being embarrassed and ashamed, Mom did not tell anyone and continued to hide her pregnancy and attend school each day. After the morning sickness subsided, she starved herself in hopes no one would notice the protruding baby bump that slowly grew in her tiny, frail body. Mom lived in fear each day of her family's reaction. She was quite aware that "messing around" was unacceptable in the eyes of her parents.

One day, Dr. Gak stopped at Mom's house to treat one of her ill brothers and nonchalantly asked how Helen was doing. Her mother questioned his comment and Dr. Gak proceeded to tell her about Helen's pregnancy. Grandma told Grandpa and he was furious with the shameful news. He drove to school and immediately had Mom removed from class, scolding her all the way home.

The only right thing to do was for Dad to marry my mother, but when the family approached Pastor Erwin Baker of the Onondaga Hill Presbyterian Church, where Mom attended her whole life, he refused to marry them because she expected a child. Dad's mother, Grandma Katherina, asked her pastor at the St. Paul's Lutheran Church in the city of Syracuse and he agreed to marry them on February 4, 1942. Paul Ramsden, who was dating Jane Wadsworth, Mom's first cousin, stood up for them. After the ceremony Mom and Dad spent the night at Grandpa and Grandma Tilden's home. The next day, still angry and disappointed with Mom's pregnancy, Grandma Grace threw Mom's clothes and pillow down the stairs, shouting at my mother when she left. The stabbing words rang out at my mom: "You made your bed, now lay in it!"

Mom delivered a very tiny baby girl on April 21, 1942. She lacked the prenatal care needed, and along with starving herself to hide the pregnancy for such a long time, the baby died two days later, on April 23th. She was named after her two grandmothers, Katherina Grace. According to hospital policy, Mom was never allowed to see or hold Katherina Grace or leave the hospital to attend her graveside service held at the South Onondaga Cemetery. My dad's parents, Grandma and Grandpa Luchsinger, took care of the arrangements and expense of the funeral, which was attended by both families.

Helen and Hank's first few weeks of married life were occupied with emotional pain and shameful rejection. At the age of sixteen, Mom had been forced to drop out of high school because she was pregnant. She was not allowed to complete her senior year, even though she only had only a few months left. Her parents, outraged, had refused to support her pregnancy. The long-time pastor of their church had refused to marry them. Behind closed doors, Mom experienced intense sorrow over the baby's death, but there were no counselors or professional services to help her with the emotional pain of losing her first child. She had no opportunity to see her baby, hold her, or attend her burial – unbearably adding to her aching heart and mental agony.

Mom and Dad lived with Grandpa and Grandma Luchsinger for a short time while looking for a place of their own. Mom tried to finish high school; however, she was too far behind to pass needed subjects such as physics and French. Dad looked for another job, even though there was work on the farm. My parents were desperately in need of being independent – out on their own – a few weeks after the loss of their child. But though unhappiness had marred their early time together, bright skies, and a bright future, were headed their way.

Chapter 8

Working at Forward Farm

With his growing knowledge of farming, a strong work ethic, and the need to provide for my mother, Dad took the offered opportunity to work at the Willard and Herbie Forward Farm near Marcellus, not far from home. Newly married, Dad needed a steady job, and the Luchsingers had a reputation of being tough, hard-working farmers – a lesson learned from immigrant parents. The job paid $40 a week plus a small furnished tenant house – not a bad salary in 1942. Farmhands who were ambitious and experienced were a premium, and at only nineteen, Henry was both.

The Forward brothers did have a small dairy farm, but most of their income came from raising chickens, eggs, and crop farming. Days started early, before five a.m., with Dad feeding and milking fifteen cows, and then again in the evening. He had one milking machine which made the job a little easier than milking all by hand.

After milking, and with the help of two other steady farmhands, Dad had the responsibility of feeding 6,000 to 8,000 chickens housed in a three-story chicken coop the size of a barn. The factory-sewed burlap bags of chicken mash, each weighing one hundred pounds, were carefully sliced open with a knife and poured into oversized galvanized pails. Pacing himself, Dad hiked up three flights of stairs to the top floor, carefully balancing the cumbersome pails. Endless trips completed the job. Water was piped in using floaters (to regulate the level of water) so the chickens never went without water. Besides feeding chickens, Dad had the daily job of gathering eggs and placing them carefully in wire baskets. He was given all the cracked eggs he wanted, in addition to his pay.

Depending on the season, after morning chores Dad would be in the fields driving tractor, planting wheat, corn, and peas, cutting hay, or cultivating. One hundred acres of potatoes were planted along with countless acres of peas. At harvest time, he would use the mowing machine to cut the pea vines, and using a pitchfork, the peas were loaded onto the farm truck and delivered to the processing plant, vines and all.

During the harvesting of one hundred acres of potatoes, Dad used a potato digger behind the tractor. Fifteen to twenty Italian women from Solvay were hired to pick up potatoes at three cents a bushel. The days were long, and the work was tough, but my dad endured to provide for his family.

Mom was expecting another child during their stay at the Forwards. This news was welcomed after their sad loss a few months before. Henry James Jr. was born on March 20, 1943, just eleven months after they lost their first child two days after birth.

Dad worked throughout the winter at the Forward Farm;

Working at Forward Farm

however, there was a little less activity as snow and blustery winds kept him in the barn or tenant house when he wasn't caring for chickens or animals.

When spring arrived, Dad continued to milk and feed the cows and tend to the chickens; feeding, watering, and collecting eggs. Additional duties were required in the fields, and plowing, cultivating, and planting made for long exhausting days. His day started before sunrise and ended at 8 or 9 o'clock in the evening. He came in the house for breakfast, lunch, a short power nap, more field work, a repeat of morning chores, dinner at six, and then another hour or two in the fields. He learned from an early age to work hard but pace himself during those long grueling days.

During this time Mom did not see much of Dad. At seventeen, she attended to her new baby, and stayed busy of keeping house, and preparing hardy meals. Mom loved to bake, and made pies and cookies for Dad along with preparing meals with meat, potatoes, and vegetables twice a day. Even though they had lots of free eggs, Dad preferred his oatmeal, toast, jam, and coffee for breakfast. Occasionally, Mom would fix some bacon, eggs, and potatoes with onions, fried crispy from leftover potatoes.

Dad loved the fresh air, riding on the old tractor or driving a team of workhorses, the seasons of the year, and experiencing success growing crops. In his heart, he knew someday he would have his own farm. But little did he know that his dream would come sooner than expected.

Working at Forward Farm

Chapter 9

Willowbrook Farm

Near Onondaga Hill, a few miles from the city of Syracuse, a large two-story six-bedroom house was built in 1795. This well-positioned home on a small incline has one side facing an enormous hill and a creek running through the property at the bottom of the hill. During the spring, water runoff from the hillside filled the stream until it overflowed its banks along a rarely-traveled dirt road. The original hand-hewn stringers, (structural beams) made of long straight maple logs, still hold up this house some two hundred and twenty-five years later.

My mother's grandparents, John and Laura Belle Wheadon Tilden, bought this old established farm – sight unseen – in 1917, at a foreclosure auction at the Court House in Syracuse. Their son Brad (born on January 1, 1900) was just seventeen when World War I broke out, and fearing that their only child would be drafted; my great-grandparents bought the farm to prevent having their only child sent off to war. Farm boys were exempt from the military so they could work the farms to feed our country. My grandfather Brad worked the farm for his father John, who was employed with the

New York Central Railroad, and planned to farm after retiring.

1904
Willet Bradley Tilden (Mom's Dad)
Laura Belle Wheadon Tilden (Mom's Grandma)
John Bradley Tilden (Mom's Grandpa)

After Grandpa Brad married my grandmother, Grace Wadsworth, in 1924, they moved to a home just a few hundred yards up the long steep hill to the corner of Norton and Young Roads. There they raised a family of five children: my mother Helen, who was the oldest, Brad Jr., John, Bob, and Herb.

Willowbrook Farm

Grandpa Brad (Willet Bradley Tilden) was not a farmer, but had a large garden and a few chickens, as most country people did in the 1920's and 30's. He worked at Precision Dye Cast Company along with his neighbor Ralph Abbey. They usually rode together and stopped at The Swallows, at the foot of Elmwood Hill, for a couple of beers before heading home. Grandpa Brad liked his beer.

Unfortunately, Great-Grandpa John Tilden died unexpectedly at the age of seventy-one after having an emergency appendectomy in the fall of 1943. He had been dressed and ready to come home from his hospital stay – then stood up, fell onto his bed, and died. There was no confirmed diagnosis, but probably death was the result of a blood clot, internal bleeding, or heart attack.

Grandpa Brad and his son Brad, Jr., at the age of fifteen, attempted to keep the original Tilden farm operating, however, it was unsuccessful. As my Dad explained, "They lacked desire, motivation, and farming experience. All three are needed to be a good farmer."

Great-Grandma Tilden, a neat, meticulous stout woman in her mid-sixties, approached my dad with an offer – she wanted my parents to move into the six- bedroom farmhouse with her and take over the farm. Dad was then a tenant at the Forward farm working for someone else, and winter was approaching. There would be no required field work there, just the daily chores of feeding thousands of chickens and milking cows. This was a great opportunity. Dad would pay twenty-five dollars a month rent to farm the seventy-five acres, with taxes minimal. He believed this was a great chance for him to be his own boss and work for himself, and Dad was optimistic, that some day he would own the farm.

The farm had everything a young ambitious farmer needed: woods, a creek running through the property, grapevines, a cow barn, chicken coop, smokehouse, – even a tobacco barn, though Dad did not plan to plant tobacco. The huge square house had an open porch, six bedrooms, and two hand-dug wells. There were workhorses, milk cows, large maple trees, pastures, and rich fertile soil which was easily tillable. But what was most important, my dad had the desire, motivation, and farming experience his father-in-law and brother-in-law had lacked.

Mom was overjoyed with the idea of moving onto her grandparents' farm, the Willowbrook Farm. (Great-Grandpa Tilden named it shortly after buying the farm in 1917 – an appropriate name because there were willow trees all along the creek bed running north and south.) Mom loved Grandma Laura Belle. As a young child, she would often have sleepovers with Grandma Tilden, who treated her with special care, as Mom was her only granddaughter.

Morris Freeman, a cattle dealer, gave Dad an estimate of the value for the cows. Immediately, Dad went to First Trust Bank in Marcellus and met with Bill Johnstone, the bank manager, to borrow two thousand dollars to buy the twenty-five cows and a team of horses from Great-Grandma Tilden. He sold six for beef and also brought six cows from the family farm on Bussey Road. (It was customary for each of Dad's siblings, who had their own livestock, to take them with them when they married and secured farms of their own.)

During the ruthless winter of 1943-44, Dad found one of his workhorse's dead. His brother-in-law Henry Melvin married to Dad's sister Barbara wanted to help. Henry had his own dairy farm and machinery/equipment business on River Road in Baldwinsville. He was willing to replace the dead workhorse, but due to the brutal weather Henry could only deliver the horse as far as the Schwartz farm on West Seneca Turnpike, where Dad met him with a bobsled. On his one-horse bobsled with attached frills, my dad was there waiting when the new member of the family arrived. The two-mile journey home across the snow-covered, drifted fields was anything but easy – the newly-acquired horse was tied behind the bobsled, not liking the trip, kicking and biting all the way, a fight my father would never forget. Dad realized later that the horse had never been broken to pull a wagon or wear a harness.

Good reliable workhorses were essential to any farm. The horses on the farm were in a separate part of the barn, adjacent to the cows. Dad plowed, delivered milk, and hauled manure using the bobsled, with his team of horses among other jobs requiring horses around the farm. They would pull the hay loader with the hay loose on the wagon. Hay tines were used to unload. Sometimes Dad would place a burlap bag over the horses' noses, hooked onto the bridles to slow the horses down.

Dad did not trust horses – one time he was nearly killed by one with a strong kick to the chest. He also had vivid memories from his boyhood on the farm of the difficult, dangerous job of trying to break wild horses transferred from the West. (I always wanted a horse. We had a barn, feed, hay – why not? "Because they're dangerous!" Dad repeatedly told me. "End of discussion!")

Besides workhorses, Dad used an old international 1020 tractor with steel wheels. Gas for the tractor was two cents a gallon, delivered. Dad's first new tractor was a John Deere G, which he bought two years after moving onto the farm. Everyone thought it was too big.

Dad labored endlessly, never avoiding the work facing him each day. Chores started before dawn at 4:30. Besides feeding livestock and chickens, the most important task was the tiresome job of milking twenty-five cows by hand. A milking machine cost one hundred dollars, a lot of money in those days, but with careful saving, Dad was able to put a small amount away each month, and within six months, he had one automatic milking machine. (Being frugal was a lesson he had learned from his immigrant parents.) Using one machine, and milking the other cows by hand, his daily chores of milking twice a day was reduced to half the time.

The first winter at the farm was full-blown, with rough biting winds and bitter cold penetrating central New York. Snow piled high on the coarse dirt roads, making the winding and hilly roads impossible to use. But cows had to be milked and the milk had to be delivered to nearby Syracuse in order to make money.

Dad was great at adapting to adversity. For two gruesome weeks during this freezing, snowy January, my dad got his milk to market by horse and bobsled and truck.

On these early frigid mornings, the heat from the cows would keep Dad warm while milking and feeding his livestock. He began the long day milking twenty-five cows, then had a quick bowl of oatmeal, hooked up the bobsled to his two huge workhorses. Dad carefully tied down four or five eighty-pound milk cans on the sled for the long bone-chilling two and one-half mile journey across rolling snow-covered fields to the Schwartz farm on West Seneca Turnpike where he parked his truck. January sun would just be coming up as he arrived at the neighbor's farm. Then he would transfer his cans of fresh milk onto his small pickup truck and head to the Bellevue Dairy on Geddes Street in Syracuse. (A few years later he shipped his milk by hired truck drivers to the Brookfield Dairy on Otisco Street. A large red number three was printed on each milk can, and these same cans were delivered back to the farm, empty, later in the day.)

Sometimes Dad picked up staples or bags of coal for the neighbors. Farmers always looked out for other people requiring assistance in those days and Dad was no exception. He was never too busy to help someone in need; sharing machinery or helping out was the Christian way of doing things.

One of those cold, snowy mornings in January, Dad had an

eight o'clock appointment with the draft board in downtown Syracuse for his physical. At twenty-one, his number had come up, as the United States was in the middle of World War II. That particular morning Dad faced a tough challenge to feed the animals, hand-milk twenty-five cows, load the bobsled, hitch the team of horses, grab a little breakfast, and travel the rough terrain – two miles over ice and snow-covered fields – all before daybreak to make his eight o'clock appointment at the recruiting center. Even though he was required to go for his physical, Dad was exempted. Farmers, according to the draft board, were needed to grow crops and produce milk to feed the country.

Living on his newly-acquired rental farm and being his own boss filled Dad with satisfaction and contentment. He was motivated to rise early on the bitter cold days, and care for his livestock like children, just as his dad had taught him. Even though a harsh winter was settling in, work was plentiful: chopping firewood for the wood cook stove, shoveling coal for the furnace, milking twenty-five cows by hand, fixing equipment, grocery shopping, and other routine duties. The farm, just a few miles from Syracuse was an ideal location for both shopping and selling produce, though most needs were met on the farm.

Meal planning was simple. Dad raised pigs, smoking the bacon and ham in the red brick smokehouse only a few feet from the back door of the house. He had his own beef, butter, milk, and eggs. Sometimes Dad's Jewish friend Morris Freeman, who had long befriended Dad, would stop by the farm on a Sunday with a leg of mutton – frequently old and strong-tasting and some large hard rolls or dried crackers to give Dad.

The farm had an enormous orchard behind the house with a variety of fruit. When Dad took the farm over, he worked hard with his green thumb to bring the dying orchard back to life. Every bit of farm produce – fruit, vegetable or animal – was either processed or sold at the market following in his father's footsteps. Mom would process beef and pork in jars with a pressure cooker. He loved the canned meat, so tasty and delicious – just like his mother prepared each fall. Dad looked forward to these savory meals throughout the winter months.

A huge garden, loaded with all kinds of vegetables, was planted and then processed using recycled canning jars. Mom and Dad were taught by example and experience. They learned the importance of planting a vegetable garden through their own frugal parents' accomplishments.

Besides chickens, Dad raised a few turkeys, some to sell and some to eat. The plump twenty-five to thirty-pound turkeys were ready to slaughter just before Thanksgiving. Fresh turkeys brought a premium price at the market at holiday time. Dad believed freshly killed was the only way to eat turkey. Wild turkeys were occasionally seen around the farm, but made tough eating and were left alone.

Grocery shopping trips were usually done along with going

to the feed mill or other needed stops. Mom would go with Dad as she did not drive until she acquired her license in the mid-fifties. (Many women did not drive during that era). The Marcellus Red and White and Ireland's store in Onondaga Hill were often used for grocery shopping or the two corner stores in South Onondaga. Purchases included staples, bologna, and sliced cheese. Flour, cornmeal to make mush, oatmeal, coffee, sugar, and molasses were staples purchased at these small independent stores. Mom and Dad were allowed to buy on credit until the milk check arrived. Meat, fruit, vegetables, maple syrup, lard, eggs and butter were produced on the farm. With a little cornmeal, sugar, flour or oatmeal, almost anything could be made to complete the daily meal with the addition of homegrown vegetables, fruit, and meat.

    Great-Grandma Tilden was a big help to Mom. She and Mom shared the housecleaning, cooking and food preservation. According to Dad, she made the best fried eggs. She never flipped an egg. After frying the bacon on the wood-burning cook stove, she used the same cast iron frying pan, dropping the eggs in the bacon fat and using a spoon, patiently coating the eggs with bacon fat until the tops of the yolks were done to perfection. She also made the best lemon pies – with freshly squeezed lemons, a costly commodity. Making a single pie took her all morning. The process had to be precise. She always used the best ingredients, including fresh eggs and lard from pig fat for the crust.

    Great-Grandma Tilden also took pleasure in entertaining her

great-grandson, Hank Jr. who never stopped investigating all the activity on the farm. She would walk with him to the barn and introduce him to a baby calf or teach him how to throw chicken feed to the roaming chickens. Also, she enjoyed watching Hank while Mom and Dad did grocery shopping or went to the feed store.

One night during the summer of 1945, the workhorses were stirring and restless all through the night in the pasture facing Great-Grandma Tilden's upstairs bedroom. After morning chores, Mom was concerned that Great-Grandma had not come downstairs. She hadn't heard a sound from her room. Dad went upstairs to her room in the front of the house to find her blankets neatly folded up to her chest, her arms crossed in front of her. On the nightstand, next to her eyeglasses, was an empty glass. (Dad said she had a glass of water mixed with baking soda every night at bed time; one-half teaspoon of baking soda in water was a remedy for indigestion.) Not a muscle had moved – at the age of sixty-six, Great-Grandma Tilden had died in her sleep.

Now Dad and Mom were on their own. They would continue to improve the farm, making it more comfortable and efficient. Dad was not only a great farmer, but proved to be a talented carpenter as well.

1946 – Mom and Hank Jr. (3 years old) pregnant with me

Chapter 10

The Old Farm Reborn

My parents' farmhouse was over one hundred years old when my great-grandparents bought the property in 1917, and after Dad moved to the farm in 1943, he was eager to remodel the 140-year-old house. The outhouse was near the back door of the old kitchen so one of the first changes Dad made was to put in an indoor bathroom, converting the pantry off the kitchen into the only bathroom of the six-bedroom house. Water was pumped from the hand-dug well behind the house, and from there, made its way to the old kitchen. Our well had a wooden cover and a submerged pump which carried water into the house through the back door.

Every farm and country home had hand-dug wells. A tripod six feet across was used to fill buckets to bring dirt out of the well. Stones, flat on one side and carefully laid, held dirt from caving in. Our second well located on the left side of our house did not provide our family with the best source of water. Often during dry, summer months we had to buy water. A large water truck would back in and drop a hose into the well, partially filling. The water only lasted a few days. Water shortage was a hardship and inconvenience to the family, but we learned to make do.

After years of struggling through water shortages, we had a new well dug in the cow pasture beside our house. Uncle Fred, Dad's brother, had the gift of witching for water (water dowser to locate water underground); he used a Y-shaped branch (twig) from a willow tree or cherry tree and held it pointed upward. When gravity (we called it magic) brought the pointed part of the branch to the ground, water could be found. He usually witched several times, making sure digging to find water in a particular location would be successful. My grandfather, John Luchsinger also had that gift, and on many occasions, he witched for water before he died in 1959. Water was so abundant and close to the surface that only a backhoe was needed to dig the hole. Once the well was dug in the center of the cow pasture, a ditch was dug and connected to the house and plumbing inside. We had refreshing cold water, all we ever needed. The old hand-dug well was converted into a septic system with leaching fields. The original hand pump is now a decoration in the front yard.

Behind the barn was a swamp hole which was eventually dug out with a backhoe, fifteen or sixteen feet deep, to supply water to the animals. A large steel watering trough with piping to the spring continually flowed with cool, fresh water. Eventually our recycled, claw-footed bathtub was used as a trough for the cows and young stock.

Soon after Dad's arrival on the farm he had transformed the pantry off the old farm kitchen to our bathroom and made a space for a wringer washing machine and installed a tub. Years later, an automatic washer and dryer were put in the bathroom and the clotheslines hanging from tree to tree were removed except one, so Mom could hang out her bed sheets. After Great-Grandma died, the old kitchen was left as a storage room and a large kitchen was created by combining the den and first floor bedroom. The door to the cellar was reversed from the old kitchen with a new door entering from the present kitchen.

For many years, the storage room (or junk room, as we called it) held a crude chest freezer modified from a milk cooler. It kept our meat, vegetables, bread, and ice cream frozen. A little later, Dad purchased an upright freezer for the cellar which had shelves that held neatly arranged bags of frozen corn, beans, and peas from the garden, jars of jam, and day-old bread Dad bought inexpensively, twenty loaves at a time. When it was time to butcher a cow, space was limited in the freezer. Meat was plentiful, especially beef, pork and venison.

In the early 1960's Dad transformed the old kitchen (storage room) into a large bedroom for our parents along with a built-in closet. After Mom and Dad moved to their new bedroom on the first floor, Karen and I took over their old bedroom. We were lucky as we had the only closet in all the bedrooms upstairs.

Behind the house was a large orchard of apple, cherry, and

pear trees but as years went by the neglected orchard disappeared from the landscape. A chicken coop, turkey pens surrounded with wire, and pig pens where also behind the house and were convenient to reach any season of the year with food and water. The back of the house also had an unsightly open dump where we burned trash.

Dad raised several pigs and fattened them up by feeding them scraps of potato peels, unused garden vegetables, and corn. If a particular pig looked thin, Dad would feed it a long piece of charcoal, to kill the worms. Sometimes the pigs were fed day-old bread and baked goods from Kellfelz Bakery on Geddes Street. Grasping the opportunity to buy cheap feed at the bakery to fatten the pigs, Dad would buy the old bread for one or two cents a pound and bring it home in burlap sacks. We watched a large man at the bakery punch a hole in each wrapper before allowing Dad to fill the feed bags. (The ripped bag would prevent anyone from reselling the bread at another location.) Sometimes the bread and baked goods, especially chocolate covered donuts, would be okay for us to eat.

For many years, the lonely maple tree across the road from the farmhouse was a symbol of the yearly killing of pigs, an unpleasant reality of growing up on a farm. Our home was surrounded by maple trees, but this one in particular was where my dad would slaughter pigs. Dad had learned the skills of butchering, cleaning, and processing farm animals from his father as a young boy. Killing animals was often witnessed by farm children – a part of life we never enjoyed, but, accepted. Dad did not want the younger children watching the killing of pigs, but we would sneak a quick look from the large dining room window. On a cool fall day, Dad would slaughter his pigs and sometimes, (for a small fee of $2.50 each, or a trade for the heart and liver) butcher pigs at the same time, for two or three local farm families. After shooting the pig with a 22 bullet or using a heavy mallet or hammer to the skull, the slaughtered pig would be lifted with a chain attached to the tree, the entrails removed, and the pig washed out. Pork was a staple for winter for many families, including our own.

After slaughtering, a fire would be made and a large round cast iron kettle (the very same iron kettle now filled with colorful flowers in the front yard) would be filled with water and heated from a wood fire and used for dipping the pig to soften its hide and hair. One by one, the pigs would be lowered down into scalding water, raised back up quickly, using a hog scrapper to shave the hair off. Heavy-duty chains held the slaughtered pigs from the large maple tree overnight to cool before processing.

The next day, the pork would be cut up on a crude make-shift table for the freezer. Dad would have a large kettle set aside to collect the extra fat. Shiny white freezer paper was used to wrap the meat. On the exterior of each package was written information clearly identifying the contents. My father would bring the fat from the slaughtered pigs into the house for Mom to process into lard. She would cook down the fat until it was liquid and pour it into small crocks, where it would cool and thicken for baking and frying in the winter. Lard made wonderful pie crust.

Old Kitchen Hand Pump and Cast Iron Kettle

Throughout our lives the old farm buildings changed along with the landscape. The original square house was updated several times in the past seventy-five years. The large open porch was enclosed in the sixties, a porch was added off the new kitchen, and later a two-car garage was added onto the porch. Additions were made to the barns as our dairy farm expanded. Corn cribs were built. An old tool shed next to the road was torn down.

Dad was a talented carpenter and did most of the remodeling himself during slow seasons on the farm. His days were long, but the needs and wants of a loving family made his home his castle. Others were not so fortunate – WWII brought others to work on the farm who were not working for themselves.

Chapter 11

Free Labor, Not Free

During the Depression in the 1930's, a government agency, the Civilian Conservation Corps (CCC), developed jobs to build parks on state and federal lands. Barracks were built in Fayetteville, at the present Green Lakes State Park, to house the workers for these job sites. However, during World War II, the barracks were used for German prisoners of war.

Throughout the summer and fall of 1944, my dad and his brother John, who had a farm on Bussey Road at the time, used these prisoners on their farms. Other local farmers also had the opportunity to benefit from the free labor. The only requirement was to pick up the prisoners at the camp in Fayetteville at a specified time, provide them with a hearty lunch, plenty of water, and return them back to the prison camp. Each detainee wore regular clothes and received no pay.

On a typical day, Dad rose before sunrise, fed the animals, milked the cows, and did other morning chores. He left a little after seven a.m. in his one-ton stake rack truck, for the forty-five minute drive to the barracks. Standing around, waiting for a day away from prison, twelve to fifteen German prisoners were ready to ride out to the farm. One prisoner was delegated to bring along a canvas bag with tin cups, plates and utensils to use at their noon meal and water breaks. One guard rode along, making sure each inmate appropriately obeyed instructions.

Dad would deliver them to Uncle John's farm to pick up potatoes that had been previously dug by a double-bladed potato digger. The guard sat in the house sipped coffee and ate anything Aunt Ruth had available. He never worried about the inmates escaping.

At noon, under the shade of a maple tree, lunch and a brief rest were granted to the prisoners. A hot lunch, prepared by Aunt Ruth, was delivered from her kitchen, in a large kettle to the area under the tree. A large coffee percolator, filled to the top with fresh coffee, was used to fill the tin cups. Water from the springhouse was also available. Usually there was a beef or pork stew, loaded with potatoes, onions, carrots, and a side of corn bread – Aunt Ruth made wonderful corn bread. Due to a shortage of sugar during the war, a simple dessert was prepared with fruit from the orchard sweetened with molasses, which nicely topped their noon meal. After lunch, the men would go to the springhouse and rinse off their dishes before going back to work, which made cleanup easy. Sometimes extra apples or pears right off the tree were offered to prisoners before heading back to Fayetteville at 4 o'clock in my dad's truck.

On another day, my dad would repeat the trip to Fayetteville, pick up the prisoners, frequently different men, and take them to his farm on Norton Road to fill the silo, pick corn, clean barns, and other field work before winter set in. Mom prepared a large kettle of meat stew adding garden produce, lots of bread, and cookies. Again, coffee and water were provided. Dad carried the pot across the road to the large maple tree by the silo where the inmates congregated. He did not want Mom near prisoners of war – so she stayed away. The prisoners appreciated the home cooked food that filled the emptiness in their stomachs. More importantly, they were elated to be away from the prison camp for the day.

    Dad and Uncle John never worried about prisoners escaping. The guard was there to keep them on task. Dad once said, "Where were they going? Many of the prisoners felt they had it better here than in Germany, where they probably would have been shot."

    After the war, the German prisoners were repatriated back to Germany. Maybe the experience they had on our family farms softened the war for them. Perhaps they remembered and spoke of the kindness of strangers in a strange land.

Free Labor, Not Free

Chapter 12

Chickens

Chickens were an important source of income and food on the family farm. Eggs were used for cooking and baking as well as food at breakfast. Old hens were used for chicken stew and soups. My grandparents raised chickens, sold eggs and chickens at local markets, and grasped every penny for the much-needed cash. My father's main job at the Forward farm had been feeding and gathering eggs for thousands of chickens daily. As a result, my parents were experts in raising chickens, selling eggs, and preparing chickens for food.

When Dad arrived at Great-Grandfather Tilden's farm, he inherited a three-story chicken barn, adjacent to the main cow barn, where the cows, hay, and grain were stored. There was no running water to the upper barn where the chickens were housed so Dad carried pails from the springhouse nearby, climbing up steep narrow stairs to each level. The chickens clucking loudly as he entered. He bought laying mash of finely ground corn, wheat, and additives in one-hundred-pound bags. After transferring the mash into galvanized pails, he would make more trips up the stairs, pouring the mash into feeding troughs, enough for all. The use of deep narrow troughs prevented chickens from wasting the food or contaminating the feed.

In the early years of farming on Norton Road, Dad raised three hundred New Hampshire Reds and Rhode Island Reds each year. They produce brown eggs. Dad believed brown eggs were healthier for you, and many of his Yiddish customers preferred brown eggs. (According to today's research the quality, flavor, and nutrition in white and brown eggs are the same.) Chickens were purchased as chicks and kept warm using a kerosene stove in the brooder house, a handmade Quonset hut. When the chickens matured, they were used for laying eggs and a few eaten for Sunday dinners.

Dad took advantage of having chickens to bring in extra cash, another significant lesson learned from his father. He gathered eggs in wire baskets each morning and carried them across the road to the farmhouse. After eggs were collected throughout the week, Mom had the tedious task of wiping off each egg with a damp cloth, preparing for the weekly egg route. She graded each egg, one at a time, using an egg scale and carefully inspected each with a box light, searching for blood spots. (A box light is a handmade wooden box with an electric bulb and an opening on top, the size of an egg. The light from the box illuminated the egg when Mom rotated the egg back and forth searching for blood clots – fertile egg.) Some customers preferred fertile eggs – with blood spots – and paid five

Chickens

cents more per dozen so these eggs were carefully placed in separate cartons. After weighing the eggs, they were graded and placed in cartons according to size: extra large, large, medium, or small.

Every Friday Mom and Dad traveled to Garfield, Burt, and Castle Streets in Syracuse on their established egg route. Eggs sold for fifty cents a dozen. Sometimes they would stop at G.L.F. (Grange League Federation), a farmers' co-op that sold fertilizer, feed, seed, and farm hardware located on Burnet Avenue and drop off a crate of thirty dozen. At G.L.F. Dad exchanged his eggs for credit to purchase farm needs. On the way back home, they delivered some to Reilly's Market in Elmwood. If there were any unsold eggs, Mom and Dad would travel to the auction barn near Split Rock held on Friday nights. Mom would also boil up extra eggs, and after peeling, fill a crock with brine for pickled eggs which would last a few weeks in the refrigerator and made a quick snack.

Rhode Island Reds weighed ten or twelve pounds by the time they matured into old, fat chickens and were sold to G.L.F. A large, covered Chevrolet truck (G.L.F. only used Chevy trucks) would pull up to the chicken coop, and load live chickens into the back of the enclosed truck to be delivered to the processing plant. After the chickens were killed and cleaned they were sold for chicken meat to the Campbell Soup Company.

A few years later, after enlarging his dairy herd, Dad discontinued the egg business since he needed more space for his expanding herd, rebuilding the three-story chicken barn over the

Chickens

basement of the field-stone foundation to store additional hay and straw. A moveable chicken coop, set on skids, was placed behind the house. Several times during the fifties and sixties the coop was moved from behind the house to across the road, conveniently near the cow barn. We raised chickens from chicks so we could enjoy barbecued chicken cooked over real wood chips for Sunday dinner. A few chickens were saved for fresh eggs used by our family.

Besides barbecued chicken, the best "eating chicken" were the plump ones roasted or fried crispy during the winter months as a treat for Sunday dinner. My job was to boil up the chicken pieces and drain them, keeping the stock for gravy. The pieces were then dipped in an egg and milk mixture and rolled in another mixture of flour, salt, and pepper. Our twelve-inch cast iron frying pan was heated with Crisco or lard covering the bottom of the pan one-half inch. Oil temperature had to be ideal – too hot, burnt chicken; not hot enough soggy crust. After the lard melted into hot oil, I tested the temperature with a sprinkle of water. When the oil sizzled, the chicken was dropped slowly into the hot pan. We didn't own a cooking thermometer, but practice taught me when the oil was ready to use for frying. Mom's careful instructions guided me in making the best crispy, fried chicken.

Our chickens had free range, roaming near the henhouse, eating bugs and grubs, and grain or chicken feed that was tossed around daily. They scratched at the dirt to find grubs and insects.

Every chicken farm had to have a rooster – no rooster, no

fertile eggs. Also, he was our morning alarm clock! Ours was very territorial, like all roosters – protecting the flock by not letting animals or people near; strutting, squawking, and flapping his wings to scare away intruders. Going to the cow barn, the rooster would cluck away at us, fluttering his wings and running toward us. In fear of his aggressive behavior, my sisters and I would avoid him by walking a few extra feet from him. Collecting eggs was left to my brothers or Dad, who braved the thorny problem of confronting the attacking rooster. When my sister Karen was four or five she was attacked by one of our powerful roosters in the barnyard. He was jumping and clawing at her tiny body when Dad heard her horrifying screams. Dad came out from the barn and quickly grabbed the rooster by the neck, giving it a few twists which resulted in a quick death. His words, along with a few choice swear words were, "You won't be attacking anyone again!" We had the tough old rooster for dinner the next day.

While we enjoyed frequent meals of delicious fried or roasted chicken when spring came around we also looked forward to sweetness from our maple trees – wonderful maple syrup. Bacon and eggs were great, but so were pancakes with real homemade maple syrup.

Chapter 13

Making Maple Syrup

As the bitter cold weather of winter started to wind down, and the temperature climbed above freezing during the day, but was below freezing at night, my dad would begin his yearly ritual of tapping the six or seven large maple trees lining the road and yard around our farmhouse. This seasonable chore occurred sometime in late February or early March and lasted four to six weeks until the temperature remained above freezing or the buds on the trees started to form.

Our front yard was lined with enormous maple trees that were planted around our farmhouse nearly two hundred years ago for shelter from the wind. The trees towered many feet above the height of the silos and barn and made handsome shade which gave us relief from the hot summer days. Our family had other uses for the trees besides tasty maple syrup for pancakes and maple sweetener. Mom had clotheslines attached from tree to tree, and swings were made for the kids.

We loved tagging along with Dad, just to watch him gather the sap. We dressed for the cold with carefully constructed winter garb of oversized coats, socks for gloves, and hand-me-down boots. Our father welcomed company for the extra help. He used a hand drill to manually make a hole about two inches in depth in two or three different places on the trunk of each tree. Using a hammer or mallet, he would pound a tap (sometimes called a spile) into the drilled hole, making a spigot for the sap to run into the pail. We didn't have any fancy maple syrup equipment, but used make-shift covers so the sap would stay clean, and to prevent snow or rain mixing in with the sap. The only stipulation was that the container or pail must hold several quarts of clear liquid sap. Making do with materials and supplies we had around the farm was part of our financial survival; there was no place in the budget for fancy maple syrup equipment unless we sold our products to the public and went big-scale.

Neighbors Art and Myrtle Norton had a sugar shack in the woods behind their home. We ventured out some weekend afternoon, in late winter, when a hint of spring was in the air. My brothers, sisters, and I entered the woods from Abbey Road, trudging through the snow, making the half-mile journey to their rustic shack. The Nortons graciously gave us a sample of the hot maple syrup on a cracker or piece of bread. They used horses and a bobsled to gather the sap from hundreds of maple trees. We were told they practically lived at the sugar shack throughout the six to eight-week production season, keeping the wood fire going, as they slowly simmered the sap until enough water evaporated to produce a rich amber color.

Making Maple Syrup

We did not stay long, but looked forward yearly to the trip.

Our own production of maple syrup was much simpler. On occasion, I went out to the trees to see how much sap dripped overnight; how cold or warm it was determined how much would be in the bucket. Two times a day we collected the clear liquid that resembled water. Sometimes we would run our fingers across the slow dripping spigot until enough sap came out to sample the faint taste of sweetness – a joyful delight!

The collected sap was poured into large covered containers on the unheated porch next to the kitchen to keep the sap cool until processing time. If we had an overabundance of sap, Dad used Mom's food processing canner to store the sap until she was ready for the next batch. To avoid any spoiling, within two days the sap was transferred into the oversized kettle, and the slow practice of simmering the sap would begin.

The process of boiling down the sap into syrup was tedious and took about twenty-four hours. Mom used her long deep-roasting pan covering two burners. She planned on ten gallons of sap to make one quart of syrup. Steam gathered on the walls as the sap evaporated. When the syrup started to thicken, Mom carefully observed the syrup for the right consistency; she waited for an amber color, watching to not burn the syrup. A whole day's labor would be wasted if the syrup burned. Mom dipped a spoon into the simmering syrup, and when the syrup slowly ran off the spoon, the yummy stuff was ready to process. Cautiously, she poured the hot syrup into pint-

Making Maple Syrup

size canning jars, usually obtaining a pint or two per batch. After the hot jars of syrup were sealed they were placed in the cool cellar for enjoyment for the next twelve months.

As quickly as one batch was done, Mom started another batch, creating a steam-filled kitchen while watching patiently for the sap to evaporate to the perfect golden color. Sometimes the syrup would be used typically for pancakes, hot flaky biscuits or French toast. Once or twice before the snow disappeared, we would slowly pour boiling hot syrup on fresh clean snow until crystallized, making maple snow cones, a short-lived treat enjoyed by all. We celebrated being involved and shared with enthusiasm and excitement of our end product.

Making maple syrup by gathering sap from the front-yard maple trees was a delightful memory of our family farm. Another treasured memory was berry and cherry picking.

Farmhouse with 200 year-old Maple tree

Making Maple Syrup

Chapter 14

Berries and Cherries

Just about the time school ended for the year, fruit around the farm started bearing sweet lush berries. A few strawberries grew in the wild, in the fields, along the edge of the hedgerows, or along the ditches. Picking the small, wild strawberries was a tedious job, and my sisters and brothers could not pick enough to make a batch of jam. Most of the time, we would come across a cluster of strawberries and eat until we grew weary and our hands were a sticky red mess.

A staple around our house was jam and toast. Whenever anyone was hungry my mother would say, "Have some toast and jam." We made nearly one hundred pints each year. In order to have enough berries to make jam, Mom and Dad traveled to Sebastian Schmidt's farm on Buckley Road, long-time family friends from Switzerland. My parents either bought or picked two sixteen-quart flats of flawless strawberries. During the second or third week of June, I would come home after my end-of-year exams to the endless task of hulling quart after quart of freshly picked berries. Mom and I worked as a team, making batch after batch of strawberry jam.

    My job was to measure out, in a large Tupperware bowl, exactly seven cups of sugar, and set it aside ready to pour into the deep cast iron kettle. After washing and removing the green stems from two quarts of berries, I chopped up the hulled strawberries with a hand food chopper, and then crushed them with a potato masher. A package of Sure-Jell was added to the kettle along with the berries. The mixture had to boil for one minute before adding my carefully measured sugar, and then stirred continuously until the jam boiled for one more minute. I would count ten more seconds before removing the jam off the stove, just to make sure the jam would firmly set up. A tad of butter was added. We skimmed off the foam, which was saved in a cereal bowl for sampling on bread later in the day. The last step was to pour the scalding hot jam into sterile glass pickle, olive, and peanut butter jars with covers which we saved throughout the year and reused. We did not have money for fancy jam jars.

    When the jam cooled, we wiped off the jars with a wet cloth, matched up the lids with the jars, and stored them for winter in our chest freezer in the cellar. What berries not made into jam were washed, hulled, sliced, and placed in the freezer for shortcake in winter months. Mom liked freezing the jam because it was easier – no need to purchase wax to melt and pour on top to seal. Furthermore, the freezer jam stayed bright red in color. Once opened for family use, the jam was stored in the refrigerator; taking only a few days before the jar would be emptied.

    Around the Fourth of July sour cherries were next to be harvested. Picking was the most fun, but processing the worst job. We had two cherry trees in our orchard behind the house which had been there for years. They lacked pruning and were very old, and as a result did not produce well. But our neighbor Ernie had an orchard filled with abandoned cherry trees left for the birds to enjoy. We never asked Ernie if we could pick his cherries; we were afraid he might say no! In our minds, we were not stealing – good-looking, tasty cherries should never go to waste. So, we pilfered them. Mom and Dad apparently knew we picked them without permission but looked the other way. Three or four of us ventured up the long, steep hill from our farm, passing Grandma Tilden's home, toting our homemade pails made from metal Crisco cans with wire coat hanger handles. About three hundred feet before reaching Ernie's farmhouse we jumped the steep ditch and climbed the vertical bank to tall, overgrown dry grass. When we got closer we kept low, slithering on our bellies in the towering grass, keeping our voices to a whisper and hiding from view of Ernie's home. Flat on our backs, we quickly filled our buckets with plump sour cherries from the low hanging branches, popping a few juicy cherries into our mouths as we picked. Without talking, we slowly slid across the tall grass, again on our bellies, with our abundance of fruit, and carefully moved down the steep bank on our butts onto the road, trying not to spill any of our precious cargo. We stopped for a quick hello at

Grandma Tilden's house, and sometimes Grandma would give us each a half-stick of gum. Other times she would apologize because she didn't have any gum or candy. After the brief visit, we would continue down the long hill back to our farm.

Then the endless job of pitting cherries began, which truly was the pits! We sat in our front yard, under the shade of the colossal maple tree, inspecting each cherry, looking for worms before putting them in the kettle. (Sometimes we would find a white, wiggly worm. Yuk! As we quickly discarded this uninvited guest, we wondered how many wormy cherries we ate while picking!) We seemed to hull thousands of cherries before having enough for a couple of pies. But the end result was Mom's wonderfully delicious flaky, two-crusted tart, cherry pies. Mom made pies and froze the remaining cherries for pies in the winter.

The last phase of our ambitious summer berry picking was the blackberries. The season would start around July 15th, and if we had a rainy season they were sweet and plump. If the summer started out dry, the berries were small and tasteless. Our hedgerows were filled with wild blackberry bushes, free for the picking to any willing individual.

But blackberry picking was difficult, a miserable undertaking. Before heading out on our picking excursion we dressed for the occasion – sturdy shoes with socks, long pants, and a long-sleeved shirt for protection. However, being July, who wants shoes, socks, long pants, and long-sleeved shirts? We never used mosquito repellent, either – I never learned this preparation would save me from being eaten alive by mosquitoes.

Mom challenged us to pick at least six quarts of the sweet luscious blackberries, sending us on our way with the same homemade pails we used for cherry picking. Our day began before the weather became sweltering hot, and also to get us out of the house for the morning. We had to walk a mile to the hedgerows along the fields, in the scorching July sun to find the best picking. (Sometimes neighbor kids would beat us to the best spots.) To reach our destination, we climbed over and under barbed wire fences, sometimes being shocked and literally thrown on our butts, not aware the electric fence was turned on! Frequently, we found ourselves tripping in the tall hay yet to be cut, tumbling while climbing ancient rock fences, or being slapped in the face from low branches as we journeyed there and home. When we became thirsty, we would lie on our bellies and suck up cool refreshing water, using our hands as cups, from the creek that ran through our property. We took no water or snacks with us. We carefully carried home our hard work, protecting the tin pails from spilling. Trudging home hot, sweaty, scratched (sometimes bleeding), and tired was the norm. After hurting for days, the soreness and aches eventually faded. We still picked several more times a season.

Weekly homemade fruit pies and jars of jam were staples at our family table. Four quarts were needed for two batches of blackberry jam, plus a heaping quart for a ten-inch blackberry pie.

Mom's crust was made with Crisco or lard, flour, and salt. For the filling, she combined the washed berries with three-fourths a cup of sugar, a little lemon juice, (if she had it), two heaping tablespoons of flour, a dash of salt, and nutmeg. Then she filled the crust with the berry mixture adding dollops of butter on top before arranging the second crust on top. The last quart was for dessert for lunch in small bowls with milk and sugar, or with cereal the next morning. Nothing tastes more delicious than a warm blackberry pie with vanilla ice cream or the sweetness of blackberry jam on morning toast!

    Our hard work as young children built character and gave us practice in persevering. Breathing the fresh air, walking the open fields, observing the birds and wild animals, – have made memories that have lasted a lifetime. But not all memories of life on the farm were pleasant. We had to share the farm, not only with our docile farm animals, but with many unwelcomed little guests who were also concerned with a place to live and enough to eat.

Chapter 15

Unwanted Critters

Seasons on our farm seemed to change as rapidly as the weather. Summer haying season ended and the corn crop was harvested. The barn was filled to the brim with hay, a bin each of oats and wheat, and two silos were packed with chopped corn silage for winter feed. Days were shorter; brisk coolness in the air reminded us that winter was not far away. As the fields became dormant, tiny, harmless gray mice found a new home within our farmhouse.

One of my greatest fears (besides the rooster and bull) was the swift-moving little creatures who ventured out at night, scurrying around the quietness of the house in search of a morsel of nourishment. Making their way throughout the peaceful six-bedroom house, they were our first clue that winter was on the way. Out of the corner of my eye, I would see the fat gray mice running along the baseboard in our country kitchen. Without hesitation, I would jump onto the nearest chair or couch, screaming.

Activity was worse in the bedroom I shared with my sister Karen. As soon as the house was silent I could hear these dreadful speed demons scampering across the tile floor of our bedroom, making a scratching noise as they traveled. Quickly I would cover my head in fear a mouse would (somehow) crawl in bed with me. This awful (though irrational) thought still haunts me to this day.

After hearing our frightened screams and yells, our fearless Dad came to the rescue. He set a couple of wooden traps with tiny bits of cheese, and strategically placed them along the baseboard of our room. Lights out! Within minutes, in the darkness of the silent bedroom, scratching and chewing would begin again, and the sound of mice feet swiftly running along our bedroom floor – then a loud snap! "Yes!" Karen or I would shout. "We caught a mouse!" Our voices were loud enough for Dad to hear from the downstairs bedroom, and he responded patiently coming up the stairs, taking the dead mouse out of the trap and resetting it. Sometimes there would still be life in the little creature lying in the trap, which Dad swiftly took care of with a quick whack on the hard floor. He left the bedroom hanging onto the tail of the unwanted visitor. After the newly baited trap was prepared, we would start the process again. Quietly lying in bed, we waited for the parade of mice to start their nighttime ritual. Snap from the mousetrap! Another yell from us and Dad was up the stairs, emptying the trap, this time grumbling as his much-needed sleep was disturbed again. Sometimes trapping mice was repeated over two or three nights but usually by mid-November killing mice would come to an end.

Fear of mice never left me. To this day, I am the first to leap

Unwanted Critters

up on a chair if one enters a room unannounced. Dad patiently came to our rescue, again and again, lost sleep, and did what was needed to remove the unwanted critters from our home. But, of course, mice won't really hurt you. A bull, however...

Chapter 16

The Bull

The family bull sent chilling fear down the spines of farm children. We were taught to keep our distance, don't ever torment him, don't wear red, and – most important – never look the bull in the eye. Terrified that our strong Jersey bull might be out of his stanchion, I never went to the barn without an adult. Some of my most vivid nightmares were of me running from a charging bull.

On occasion, I was asked to go to the milk house, adjacent to the cow barn, with our one-gallon tin pail to get milk for the noon meal. My routine was to go to the hay hole on the second level of the barn near the grain shoot, open up the latch, lie on my belly, hang on tight to the sides, and lower my head down as far as I could see. "Yes, the bull is where he should be," I would say to myself with relief.

Comfortable knowing the bull was securely tied up in his stanchion; I sprinted to the milk house with my empty pail. With all my power, I removed the partially filled ten-gallon galvanized steel can of milk floating in ice cold water of the cooler, set the can on the concrete floor, and shook the heavy can to mix up the rich Jersey cream that had settled on top. With a little tug I removed the cover, taking hold of one of the handles with all my strength, using my knee and thigh for balance, and poured the milk into my pail. Without dilly-dallying, I placed the cover securely back on the large milk can and with much difficulty lifted the can back into the cooler, keeping one eye on the milk house door, just in case the bull decided to find me. Since I always spilled a little milk while pouring, I washed the floor using the black rubber hose attached to the faucet, forcing the white murky water down a drainage hole in the corner of the milk house.

Without any more delay, I then ran swiftly back to the house, carefully carrying the tin can filled with cold milk for our noon meal. The whole process took only a few short minutes but seemed like hours. All the time I was collecting the milk, I was thinking that possibly the bull would stick his head in the milk house door, charge, and leave me with no place to run!

I clearly remember a July day, warm and sunny, when I was about twelve or thirteen, Mom told me – you were told, not asked – that she needed milk for the noon meal. The usual dread filled my body. Oh no, a trip to the barn! I went through my ritual of first going to the hay hole, lying on my belly, hanging onto my eye-glasses with one hand, and slowly and carefully looking through the hole to check on the bull. But this particular day I was dumbfounded to see the bull's large, brown, glaring eyes looking directly up at me, happily chewing his cud from the grain shoot next to the hay hole!

The Bull

He was not in his stall! Instead he had somehow managed to get loose and at the base of the grain shoot. More frightening was the thought that the bull could conceivably get out of the barn after he filled his belly.

    Quickly I jumped up, running as fast as my legs would go across the road, dropping the tin pail while taking brief glances back fearing the bull was chasing me. As I got closer to the house, I started screaming, "The bull is out! The bull is out!" Shortly after, my dad came home from field work for the noon meal; I blurted my breathtaking news, which he took in stride. He quickly went to the barn, walked up to the bull, easily harnessing the contented animal that had been eating sweet grain all morning, and placed him back in his stanchion.

    So, we did not lack excitement, even danger on the farm. But there were some quiet, peaceful days – especially Sundays.

Chapter 17

Summer Sundays

Farm work never ended. Seven days a week, fifty-two weeks a year. No sick days, no holidays, no vacations. However, on our farm, Sunday was special. Our mother didn't approve of Dad harvesting crops or baling hay on Sundays, just allowing him six or seven hours to feed livestock and milk cows. Mom would remind Dad that God wanted us to take it easy on Sunday, and she knew he needed the rest. On a few rare occasions crops were harvested on Sunday. The hay needed several consecutive warm, dry days, and if we had a rainy summer, Dad would bale hay on a hot, sunny Sunday when the hay had properly dried.

Sunday dinner was unique each week. Preparation started on Saturday after evening chores. Dad would go to our round, dome-shaped henhouse behind the farmhouse and select four or five young chickens (pullets), placing them squawking in a feed bag. Each weighed two and a half to three pounds, the best size for barbequing.

My brothers and sisters congregated to watch with wide-open eyes as Dad took the heavy-duty ax and flat block of wood from the barn and placed them outside the milk house. (Other times chickens were killed on the side of the house, where the headless chickens ran down the bank, spraying blood everywhere.) Killing them was quick and painless. Dad placed each chicken on the block of wood, and then made a powerful blow with the ax to the neck. After the head fell to the ground, the headless chicken would shake and flutter, spraying blood. Sometimes Dad wouldn't get out of the way quickly enough and blood would splatter on his pants. Other times the chicken kicked and moved so fast that Dad lost his grip on the legs, and the headless chicken floundered all over the barnyard until it finally keeled over dead. The old saying "You act like a chicken with its head chopped off" vividly compares such behavior, of a chicken running around every which way, with how a person might act when completely unstable mentally, emotionally, or physically.

    Boiling hot water in a galvanized pail was ready, and each chicken was swiftly dipped in and out to remove the feathers; with little effort, the feathers then peeled off and only a few feathers had to be plucked. We stayed our distance, watching intently the drama in the barnyard – the thought of chickens dying today and dinner tomorrow made us cringe, but we understood life on the farm was about birth and death.

    Within minutes Dad placed the four or five freshly plucked chickens in a pail, then set off to the kitchen where Mom's job began. She placed layers of newspapers on the kitchen counter and with a sharp knife, made a slit from the tip of the breastbone to the tail of the chicken. Carefully she removed the guts or entrails, saving the heart, and liver. Mom sliced the gizzard open, removed the grain, washed it out and placed it in the pan along with the heart and liver. She washed the chicken, split it into halves using a sharp butcher knife (sometimes a hammer), and the cleaned chicken joined the liver, heart, and gizzard. She rolled up the messy newspaper and started the process over until all the chickens were gutted, cleaned, and placed in the refrigerator ready for the grill.

1953 – One of the few family photos
Front Row from Left: Beverly, Karen
Back Row: Hank, Me, Don

Sunday mornings my siblings and I would attend Sunday school at the Onondaga Hill Presbyterian Church during the nine months church school was in session. Before leaving home, Dad would reach in his pocket for loose change for the offering, usually a nickel or few pennies. We piled into the back seat of our two-door Plymouth, stop at the neighbor farm to pick up the Isgar children, and head to church. Due to the lack of space in our church basement, some of the grades were taught at nearby homes. We walked to our classes for Sunday school lessons and headed back to church for the last few minutes, singing songs like "Jesus Loves Me" and "How Great thou Art" – songs which still remind me of our early connection with God. Sunday school teachers collected the offering we had securely placed in our pockets before leaving home, and a short biblical lesson, geared to all age groups, was led by our Sunday school superintendent, Mr. Dense. We had a closing prayer before we left for home.

After Sunday school, we waited outside for neighbor Louis Isgar to give us a ride home. We again climbed in, packed like sardines, for the five-mile trip back home. Younger siblings sat on the laps of older ones – no seat belts to keep us out of harm's way.

Seldom did we miss Sunday school. Mom and Dad were committed to making sure we all attended regularly, received our Bibles, and joined the church. During July and August we attended church when joint services were held with the Onondaga Hill Methodist Church.

1957 – My Family at Home
Front Row from Left: Shirley, Christine, Don
Back Row: Mom, Dad, Beverly, Me

After changing from our Sunday best into play clothes, I anticipated our very special Sunday dinner with Mom and Dad and my seven sisters and brothers, a crowd by itself. Dinner was always at one o'clock. Along with the freshly killed chickens for grilling, we had parsley or salt potatoes, sometimes macaroni salad, and seasonal vegetables from the garden harvested that morning – wax or green beans, peas, and fried summer squash were the most popular, with Swiss chard or spinach on occasion. Sweet corn and tomatoes came a little later in the season.

Dessert was Mom's famous graham cracker crust pie filled

with homemade vanilla pudding with lots of meringue on top, made in a twelve-inch glass pie plate. (The dessert, along with the rest of the meal, was cost effective. We had our own rich, Jersey milk from the barn and eggs from the chicken coop.) The best part of dessert was the tradition that each Sunday a different sibling could eat from the pie dish – the last remaining graham cracker crust and creamy gooey filling in the bottom of the plate, a special treat when it was your turn!

    Mom and I made the pie on Saturday. The pie shell was easy. She placed about eight tablespoons of butter in the pie plate (melted in the oven – there was no such thing as a microwave.) Mom seldom measured exactly; she was great at eyeballing ingredients. After removing the pie plate from the oven, she added two packages of crushed graham crackers and six heaping tablespoons of sugar, stirring until mixed well. Her secret to crushing the crackers was using her rolling pin, being careful not to pop the graham cracker wrapper. She then put aside one-half cup of graham cracker mixture for the topping; she uniformly placed the crackers, butter, and sugar mixture evenly around the bottom and sides of the pie plate. This was then popped back in the oven to brown nicely. The third package of graham crackers would be hidden in the cupboard for a simple dessert at our Sunday night supper – a little confectioners' sugar, milk, and cocoa powder was made into frosting for the crackers, just enough for each sibling to have half a graham cracker sandwich for dessert.

Summer Sundays

Making the filling took all Mom's attention; as she said, "It was a little tricky." She had a two-quart double boiler for making pudding. Mom would put one and one-half cups of sugar and one-third cup of flour with a dash of salt, along with four cups of milk, in the top of the double boiler and mix well. While that was heating up, she carefully separated six eggs, making sure no yolk mixed with the whites. (She repeatedly advised us, "egg whites will not beat up if yolk is mixed in.") As the milk mixture cooked she continually stirred, making sure lumps didn't form. When it started to thicken she ladled about half a cup of the pudding and mixed it with the egg yolks then slowly added it back into the pudding in the double boiler on the stove, pouring gradually and blending well. Cooking took a couple more minutes, and then it was removed from the stove, and three tablespoons of butter and two teaspoons of vanilla were added. She let the pudding set a few minutes before pouring it into the perfectly baked graham cracker shell.

Using an electric hand mixer, Mom then beat the six egg whites until she had stiff peaks, adding four tablespoons of sugar as she mixed. She never had cream of tartar, but her meringue was perfect. After spreading the beaten whites onto the pie, she sprinkled the buttered graham crackers (set aside earlier) over the beaten egg whites, placing the pie back into the oven to brown up nicely, watching it carefully. After cooling she would place in it the refrigerator for the next day's dinner.

Mom focused on doing one chore at a time and doing the job

well. Her cooking lessons taught me how to make this homemade pie from scratch, and soon I took over the job. I eventually earned the reputation of making wonderful pies and, as an adult, made hundreds of pies for church dinners, family events and friends.

Vanilla Cream Graham Cracker Pie

Sunday morning Dad started the wood fire about eleven o'clock, making sure he allowed enough time for the wood to burn down to hot coals. If the fire was too hot, or there was too much flame, the chicken would burn. He knew how to make an ideal fire, using wood scraps from around the farm for firewood, and warned us all to stand back as he poured a little gasoline on the wood and lit it with a match. The barbeque pit was made from crude cement blocks and an old grate to hold the chicken halves. We never heard of fancy barbeque grills using propane or had money for charcoal.

Before laying the chicken halves on the grill Dad tested the fire, putting his hand over the grate; he could tell when the fire was the correct temperature. He sent one of us kids to fetch the chicken, giblets, and sauce, already prepared in a large Tupperware bowl. Mom had a special barbeque sauce recipe that the Boy Scouts used in the 1950's and 60's at their chicken barbeque fundraisers: – one quart of cider vinegar, 1 1/2 cups vegetable oil, 2/3 cup salt, four tablespoons poultry seasoning, two teaspoons black pepper, and one raw egg mixed together. This recipe made enough for the ten halves we barbequed on Sundays.

Dad carefully placed the chicken halves, gizzards, hearts, and livers on the fire. An old clean cloth securely tied to the end of a long fork would be used to baste the chicken; we never owned a basting brush of any kind. The tiny chicken hearts usually fell into the fire. The gizzards and livers would be done first, and we dipped them again in the same bowl of sauce to get that extra vinegar salt flavor. During those days, we never heard of food poisoning, and never did any family member become ill.

Chicken was done to perfection at approximately 1:00. We did not own a meat thermometer, but Dad knew when it was ready to eat – no undercooked or dried out, burnt chicken – never!! At the same time, a bowl of potatoes and several vegetables were placed on the kitchen table, and we all gathered around the kitchen table to say a blessing, and savor the wonderful meal. Scrap wood from around the farm, fresh chicken from the henhouse, potatoes and vegetables from the garden, eggs and milk for our fabulous dessert – so much to be thankful for!

Sunday afternoon was time for rest, after mounds of dishes were washed, dried, and neatly stored in our cupboard, and the kitchen floor was swept. We lay under the same large maple tree where the barbequing took place, taking pleasure in the cool, gentle breezes of summer. Dad and my brothers Hank and Don did the mandatory milking and farm chores in the evening, but the rest of us just enjoyed the lazy afternoons and evenings of our summer Sundays.

1960 – Sisters on Front Yard of our Home
Front Row from Left: Shirley, Christine
Back Row: Beverly, Karen

Just once a year we all had a very special Sunday. On that day, we took a trip to visit Aunt Ruth and Uncle John, who lived far away near the sleepy little town of Boonville, NY.

Summer Sundays

Chapter 18

Annual Vacation

Besides fabulous Sunday cookouts and the occasional baling of hay on Sunday, we never changed our routine. Vacations were just not experienced by most farm families, especially if you had dairy farms and milked cows twice daily. We were no exception. Vacation was only a word.

On Saturday night, however, sometime in July or August, Mom made a long-distance thirty-cent phone call to Aunt Ruth in Boonville, NY to see if she wanted company the next day. First "O" for operator was dialed and she was told Aunt Ruth's phone number, then we all listened intently to our side of the conversation. When the parting words were, "See you tomorrow!" we were overjoyed.

After routine chores and breakfast, we piled into our two-door Plymouth sedan, all seven, eight, or nine of us (depending on the year), and made the two-hour drive to Boonville to visit Dad's brother Uncle John and Aunt Ruth. Mom always had a baby in her arms and a little one beside her in the front seat; the rest of us were packed in the back, quietly squabbling for the window seats.

Dad kept a switch taken from a tree branch parked under the

front seat where he could quickly retrieve it, if needed. Not too often did we misbehave – we knew Dad would use the switch. With one quick motion, he would reach back and swat whoever was in the line of fire. One warning was all we needed. "You're going to get it if you don't settle down and behave! I don't want to hear a word from anyone!" he would yell sternly. We knew he would use the tree branch on us, so we behaved.

Our two-hour drive northeast took us through small towns and villages on the way to Rome, NY, then on to the scenic gorge road with mountain streams and continuous woods of pine to Boonville. The little ones sometimes sat on the laps of older kids. The front seat was one continuous bench seat, which easily allowed seating for four. Seat beats? Unheard of in the 50's.

Our first glimpse of Ruth and Johnny's place was the vegetable and fruit stand surrounded by tall pines next to the busy road. Perfectly arranged plums, peaches, and apples, bushels of sweet corn, and an array of colorful vegetables, all grown from my uncle's garden or purchased at the wholesale market in Utica forty miles away, were for sale. My uncle strived for perfection, a lesson learned from my grandfather.

Aunt Ruth made twenty dozen (240) homemade fried cakes early each weekend morning, both plain and cinnamon. We never tasted any, but watched the large glass-covered containers constantly being replenished. The donuts sold out quickly to campers heading to Old Forge and beyond in the beautiful Adirondack Mountains. A

Annual Vacation

"serve yourself" sign with a money box was available; honesty was the norm in that era, and seldom was there any cheating or thievery.

By the time we arrived at Aunt Ruth's house we were starved. We never packed snacks or had water bottles, just a baby bottle in the front seat filled with milk for the littlest traveler. Aunt Ruth prepared a large noon meal, served shortly after we arrived – usually a baked ham or pot roast, a huge bowl of buttered mashed potatoes with several bowls of fresh garden vegetables, and a pile of white bread or rolls. For dessert, she served a large 9 by 13-inch cake made from scratch with white, mile-high fluffy frosting, using lots of egg whites for the frosting and the yolks for the cake (from their chickens, of course). Every bowl was empty at the end of the meal. Aunt Ruth was a great cook! I helped with the endless pile of dirty dishes, drying and stacking. By the time dishes were done, Aunt Ruth's supply of donuts had disappeared from the stand out front. She told us the same people stopped yearly for vegetables and donuts for their camping up north.

After dinner Dad and Uncle John disappeared for the afternoon, to the potato barn and fields, or his lumber mill, a short jaunt from the house. John proudly showed Dad his progress and successes in his agricultural undertakings. Uncle John, who was fifteen years older than my Dad, once owned a home on Bussey Road, a small dairy farm with a few acres of potatoes, but he sold out in the early 1950's and moved his family to Boonville. There he established a lumber mill and potato farm with ideal sandy soil for growing flawless potatoes and vegetables. A few years later he ventured into greenhouses filled with vegetable and flower plants, dealing directly with retail businesses and local families. He also sold freshly cut Christmas trees at the Regional Market in Syracuse, and Aunt Ruth skillfully made hundreds of wreaths. They worked diligently, as a team, like my grandparents before them.

    We all liked Aunt Ruth but were a little afraid of her. She was a tall, heavy-set woman with a loud, stern voice. Mom told us she regularly used a belt to make her kids behave. (They were grown up by the time we made our yearly trip to Boonville.) Needless to say, we minded our p's and q's.

    During the afternoon boredom set in. Aunt Ruth then sent us on a wild goose chase to the fishing hole or lumber mill, and once to the old cemetery down the road. Sometimes we played in the mountain of sand near their home to pass the time. My aunt and uncle always had mean, aggressive dogs that barked continuously and were tied up outside the enclosed porch. A couple of cats were inside the house. Aunt Ruth also fed squirrels from a wooden tray attached to a ledge conveniently located outside the living room window. It was very entertaining to watch the fearless little creatures looking in at us while they ate corn or peanuts in the shell that she regularly placed on the tray.

    We left for home mid-afternoon, looking forward to our yearly stop in Oneida at a seasonal custard stand. My sister Karen and I were sent in to purchase eight small vanilla cones; Dad had a

Annual Vacation

larger twenty-cent cone. A folded-up dollar bill would buy us each a cone. No tax and no change! Stopping for an ice cream custard cone was a highlight of our trip and afterwards two of us kids would curl up on the backseat floor using the hump in the middle (the drive shaft), as our pillow. Hearing the rumble of the road and feeling the warmth of the engine would put us to sleep.

We arrived home late, usually 6:30 or after. Dad and my brothers still had to feed the livestock and the bellowing cows needed to be milked; sometimes we helped. We all went to bed that night grateful to have a day away from home and the road trip to visit our extended family.

Uncle John had learned lessons from his father about successfully growing crops and selling quality produce. We always remembered the picture-perfect fruit and vegetables carefully displayed for the public. As children we were blessed with our only family vacation, a memorable day in Boonville, and listening to the adults catching up on news and stories from home and around town, celebrating the simple but delicious foods, creative play, and the joy of family.

Farm life was arduous, our vacation day a rare treat. Keeping us all working and cooperating was difficult sometimes for Mom and Dad, and often required ... well, yes, discipline! And we all received it.

Chapter 19

Discipline

Living in a home surrounded by eight kids, rules, regulations and boundaries were the norm. Work and cooperation were essential. Managing a farm and household tasks, our parents had little patience for disrespect or laziness. Our dad had learned discipline first-hand from his father.

When our parents were provoked we were promptly disciplined. All eight of us occasionally fought, had attitudes, tried our luck at lying, and sassed or talked back. But our parents never, ever, allowed us to get away with anything – not for one minute! Mom did most of the discipline with the six girls as she usually witnessed any bad behavior. If Dad saw any of us acting out or sassing our mother, watch out! He would take his belt off and use it.

Mom claimed I was the worst when it came to sassing. Being the oldest girl, I had many duties and opportunities to talk back, but expected to be a good example for my siblings. However, I resented the fact that many of the chores around the house – like cooking, food preservation, cleaning, and ironing, were given to me while my sisters played or entertained themselves.

Once as a teenager I had to clean our kitchen cabinet filled with spices, baking needs, serving dishes, noodles, rice, etc. – everything had to be removed and cleaned, then replaced on new shelf paper cut exactly to size. I truly abhorred that dirty, tedious job every six months but Mom also hated it, so I was designated, though unwilling. On this particular Saturday, Mom started barking at me to get the job started shortly after our 8:00 breakfast. I annoyed her by moving at a snail's pace, and then made a negative comment in an inflective voice. Within seconds she said I could not go to my friend Sara's house after lunch. My sassiness began! Anger and frustration built up in me and I slammed dishes down on the counter. Mom quickly gave me a swat with the fly swatter. I burst out, without thinking, "I hate you! I wish I was never born!" I was steaming. "Oh boy, what have I done?" I thought.

Mom grabbed the wooden spoon, and there were a few hard whacks to my shoulder and behind. After a good cry daring not to say another word, I went back to work and finished the job. I was fifteen and needed to be put in my place. Nothing more was said. That day I learned you never say you hate your mother. You hit a sensitive nerve.

My friend Bonnie shared a similar story as a teenager. Her father took the hinges off her locked bedroom door, and used his belt, after she told her mother "none of your business" when her mother asked her a question. Kids don't forget those tough discipline lessons.

Discipline

Often when we misbehaved whatever was handy (hairbrush, soap, wooden spoon) was used for discipline. There were eight kids, all pushing clear-cut boundaries. Today parents are arrested for physically disciplining their children. But fifty or sixty years ago it was unwritten law – respect your parents, do as they say, obey the rules and do what you're told – no ifs, ands, or buts! Getting in trouble in school meant getting more discipline at home. A boy never had to be told to give a woman a seat on the bus; a young respectable man just did it. We had respect for each other. At home, without complaining, we were assigned farm duties and responsibilities to help things run smoothly.

Every one of my seven siblings remembers the lava soap routine. Mom washed our mouths out with a bar of lava soap after talking back. For hours, we would pick soap particles out from between teeth, sometimes spitting or rinsing out our mouths to get rid of the awful bitter taste.

The hairbrush was a handy tool for painful spanking behinds. Mom used it, I am sure, to save her from an injured hand. Grabbing our hair was quick, before we had a chance to run or defend ourselves – it was easy to grab since all six girls had fairly long hair. We knew Mom's rage, and after pushing her last button fearfully, ran out of the house before she caught us. Things settled down and were forgotten in a brief time. I can remember Mom saying, "I have had it with you kids!" Being threatened to get it, however, we never hung around to find out what it was we were going to get.

Discipline

Unwritten rules in our home were followed very closely. No lying in bed until noon as teenagers. We were up by 8:00, when Dad and my two brothers came in from finishing the morning milking for simple breakfasts most mornings – cereal, toast, jam orange juice was routine. During winter, we had oatmeal (rolled oats) or Ralston (wheat cereal); occasionally eggs or pancakes and bacon. No snacking! Farm families had three hardy meals every day. Cookies were there after school (if we were lucky) and the only beverages were water, milk or Kool-Aid in summer. We ate a healthy diet by today's standards. Fresh garden produce in summer and frozen or canned vegetables and fruits from our freezer or pantry were served every day.

Chores were clearly spelled out. We had no dishwasher – I was it! My sister Karen dried dishes. We ate what was on the table. No special meals were made; we were taught to eat what was made even when we disliked it – liver, cow tongue, Spanish rice, goulash. Whatever was cooked and served was what we ate, and no whining or showing disapproval. If you picked at your food, don't show up in the kitchen later seeking junk food – we did not have any. Occasionally, for a treat, we had popcorn made on the stove in oil. After popping, we melted butter and slowly added it to the corn, finishing with a light sprinkling of salt.

Milk was served at every meal – whole, rich, creamy milk straight from the milk house across the road. Cream was at least two inches at the top of each pitcher. Disliking the rich milk, I once reluctantly refused to drink it. Dad was so upset with my attitude that he poured a glass of milk directly from the top of the milk jug, cream and all, forcing me to drink. I gagged, cried, spit all over, and traumatized my younger siblings who witnessed the event but after that always drank some milk to appease my dad.

If we acted out at the dinner table we were threatened with being placed in the cellarway. The door was next to the kitchen table, and entry to the home of rats and mice, at least we believed that. Mealtime was for eating, not misbehaving, or you would be locked in the cellar. Our sister Beverly was placed in the landing of the cellar for a short time, but never me. Our family ate three meals together, seven days a week. Dad was strict on all of us sitting together – no hats, no bare skin, eating what you took. We stayed at the table until everyone finished their meal. This was a rule that even the youngest children followed. Dad's warnings were enough to keep us in line.

My sisters and brothers always behaved in school, as did most children those days. We would be punished again at home if we caused any trouble. Parents did not go to school as lawyers ready to sue; rules were rules and were clearly followed. We didn't talk back to teachers because we didn't talk back to parents. Respect for others was taught early and followed us through adulthood. Our parents did not question teachers but respected them and trusted the school system.

Some of our discipline mirrored how our grandparents

Discipline

disciplined our parents. Once Dad had to go to the woods after dark and bring back a bone from the remains of a cow as punishment for getting out of line. Meanwhile his sister Rosie had to go to the potato field and bring back the top of a potato plant. Rosie and Dad, not knowing the other had been sent out, passed in the dark, nearly scaring each other half to death. My brother Mort, the nickname given to Don, at eleven or twelve, had to go to our woods and fetch a bone from remains of a calf. I remember looking out the upstairs bedroom window watching him in the moonlight scared for him. Later in life he said he out foxed my dad by picking up two bones, hiding one near the house. The next time he was sent on the bone-picking mission, he hung around, timing the trip, and brought back the second bone without having to travel to the woods. That was typical of my clever brother Mort.

Another time Mort, an all-star basketball player for Onondaga Central, played a practical joke during lunch in the school cafeteria. We had salt and pepper shakers on each table, and Mort decided it would be funny to take the top off the shaker, turn the shaker upside down and carefully place the top on the bottom of the shaker. When a student unknowingly picked up the shaker, salt spilled all over the table. Teachers ate with us in the cafeteria and witnessed the shenanigans, so Mort was walked to the office for immediate discipline. His punishment was to miss the important basketball playoff game in Watertown that night! Lucky for all, the team narrowly won the game. Mom and Dad were not happy with his behavior; there was no blaming the administration or teachers. He had to take full responsibility for the trouble.

I once asked Dad if he ever got into trouble at school. "Yes," he said, once he skipped school with Gerald Hourigan, another local farm boy, to attend a farm auction. When the principal found out, they were suspended from school for a week. My father's punishment, from Grandpa, was to work every minute at home on the farm, hard labor, for the entire week, in addition to his regular chores.

If we really needed strong discipline, our parents told us they would call the police! The police would then send us to Hillbrook Detention Center if we continued to misbehave. This threat kept us all in line because we truly believed they would do it.

Discipline then, by today's standards, is looked upon by many as cruel and unusual punishment. Social services would have been at my parents' doorstep. But we were never beaten or deprived of love, only taught the importance of respect and rules to insure we learned how to become successful adults. All eight of us grew up to be responsible, law-abiding, hardworking, family-oriented citizens.

We respected and loved our parents. Maybe consistent rules and clear boundaries with a little sprinkling of corporal punishment weren't so bad after all and, of course, there were always some happy, pleasant times – like our birthdays.

Chapter 20

Birthday Barter

Living on a farm in the 1940's, 50's, and 60's with seven sisters and brothers, our food was plentiful but cold, hard cash was scarce. As my 11th birthday on August 3rd approached, a girl's bike seemed an impossible dream. We had several old boys' bikes to share, usually with no fenders, bent frames, broken pedals and plenty of rust. Riding bikes up and down our rarely-traveled gravel road, on cow paths and in open fields was relatively safe and exciting. We rode without fear of injury. The faster we rode the more we laughed. We built up endurance, muscles, and dexterity, and got lots of fresh air. When we fell off a bike, skinned a knee or tore up a heel, we hobbled home, washed the blood off, and smothered the injury with Watkins' grease, purchased from a local, overly zealous door-to-door salesman we nicknamed Smiley. Then we wrapped the wound with a crude, simple bandage made from strips from a clean old white sheet if needed. No sympathy! We learned from an early age to tough it out.

As my birthday was in summer, I never experienced the joy of passing out birthday invitations to my friends in school like other girls did, or had the whole class sing "Happy Birthday" to me. Years ago, teachers did not set aside a day for summer birthday celebrations. Mom made sure a nicely wrapped gift was on the dining room table when we got up on a birthday morning; she also served a homemade two-layer birthday cake with ice cream at dinner. None of my sisters or brothers remembers having birthday parties with their school friends – sharing our birthday with siblings and parents was sufficient.

When I awoke that August 3, 1957 morning and walked down the steep stairs which lacked a railing, from my upstairs bedroom, I met with an unforgettable surprise. Breathtaking excitement surged through me. For there, parked in the archway between the living and dining rooms, was a shiny, red, girl's two-wheeled bike with front basket, light, and flat rear bicycle rack! (The flat rack was important because I could give my younger siblings a ride.) The bike was a perfect size! No need to share the old beat up boys' bikes any longer!

Later that day I found out that the bike had belonged to Joyce Gilson. Her mom and dad, Dorothy and Ernie Gilson, had a small farm two roads from us, needed to have their hay cut for their pony and cow. She was three years older than me, never rode the bike, and agreed to part with it, so an agreement was made between Dad and Ernie to trade the bike for Dad's cutting and baling the hay.

In addition to my new bike I received two large bags of expensive clothes Joyce had outgrown just in time for the start of sixth grade in a few weeks. Joyce was an only child, and I would happily receive all her hand-me-down clothing from time to time. Included in the bags were two wool plaid skirts and sweaters to match. My heart was filled with gratitude. The biggest delight was a red, very stylish full-length winter coat with large black buttons which I wore two winters.

In my mind, Joyce had everything – nice clothes, her parents all to herself, and anything she wanted. She didn't have to do anything, while I, even at eleven, had countless chores and numerous responsibilities. Her parents even drove her to a private school. But looking back, I was the one who had everything – plenty of obligations and activities, and many teachable moments on the farm. We were taught to be patient, wait our turn, share, and dream about what was beyond our means. These were important values and lessons that farm kids from large families learned at an early age. I would not trade the memories, laughter, and challenging work that encouraged creativity that we experienced during that era for anything.

Grandpa Luchsinger had come to America with dreams. He had to make deals, barter, and sell his goods to make an honest living for which his family was thankful. My dad also used and traded his skills so his family could have memories that would last a lifetime. Most of those memories were pleasant ones, certainly. Living on a farm provided endless opportunities for playtime.

Birthday Barter

Chapter 21

Playtime and Pets

As young children, we didn't lack for entertainment. If we suggested we were bored Mom would give us a job – picking beans, folding laundry, cleaning our rooms, sweeping a floor, making a pie, or dressing our little sisters. Work was endless with eight kids. In order to avoid a "job" we found something to do. Our imagination ran wild, spending hours enjoying the simple pleasures country living offered.

Playing house was one of our favorite pastimes. Every young girl wanted to play house and role-play a family. Someone was selected to order the kids around playing the role of the stern father. Dolls were scarce; however, younger siblings and babies were plentiful! Mom allowed us use of her old, plastic Melmac dishes that had lost their bright red, blue, orange, or yellow color. From the kitchen, we took plastic Tupperware cups, a few play dishes, tin pie plates, and an old pot or pan which all enhanced creative play. The only stipulations were to bring everything back to the kitchen and pick up the yard when we finished.

Getting dirty never crossed our minds. My sisters and I

pulled up grass, pretended to cook, took water from the kitchen sink, and made mud pies with small pebbles placed carefully in wet dirt. If Dad was available we pled with him to build a makeshift table from scraps of wood or discarded plywood and put a few nails in the wood to make a crude little table. We didn't care – we made do and were happy with what we had. Tree stumps made perfect chairs. With old dishes, water, dirt and scraps of lumber we were able to fill our mornings with pretend playing, fun, and laughter.

    On rainy days we entertained ourselves playing school on our large open porch – no screens or windows, but the porch was big enough to keep us dry. Even if rain appeared we continued to play and gentle breezes in summer kept us cool. Being the oldest I was the teacher. Two old school desks with flip-up tops were given to us by Doris Hallstead, the owner of the one-room schoolhouse located a few hundred feet up the road. We played for hours until we had enough grades in arithmetic, writing, reading, and spelling. My goal as teacher was to obtain enough grades from all those tests I gave out to make a report card for each of my three or four sisters who might play. Our meager supplies included a few broken crayons leftover from the school year, pencils sharpened with a knife, and scrap paper or trimmings from a wallpapering project. Books were limited to nice ones given to us at our Sunday school. Many days were enjoyed and good memories made on our porch.

    Sometimes during hot summer afternoons, we ventured into the muddy creek a few hundred feet away to swim. The murky water was only a couple of feet deep but the spring-fed water was cool and refreshing. We dared each other to enter the three-foot-round culvert which went under the road and exit on the other side. (Fear of seeing a snake or snapping turtle prevented most of us from taking the dare.) Sometimes the banks of the creek contained six inches or more of dark, muddy muck; our feet oozed deep into the mud, sometimes up to our ankles. Washing it off was no problem – we walked a few feet to clean water and watched the mud on our legs and feet slowly fade away.

    Frogs were plentiful. Butterflies and wildflowers, especially daisies, black-eyed Susans, and yellow buttercups, covered the banks. Willow trees lined the creek bed all the way to the woods. Halfway to the woods was a pond dug by Uncle Pete Luchsinger using his John Deere Dozer 40. We avoided the frogs, muck on the bottom, and meadow weeds where snakes hid. We swam in the pond for a couple of years, before it became overgrown with algae, cattails, and weeds. Then the cows used the pond as a source of drinking, and after a few years it disappeared.

    A few tall slender cattails grew in one corner of the creek near the road. In the spring, we would catch pollywogs and bring them home in glass peanut butter jars filled with creek water for the day. Unfortunately, by the next day they were dead, floating on the top of the water.

    We played hopscotch (a game with marked squares) on the cement walkway Dad poured one summer from the kitchen entrance.

Playtime and Pets

It was just big enough to make all the individual squares required for the game. We vigilantly saved the one or two pieces of chalk we owned until we played hopscotch again. Dad took joy in planting colorful pansies next to the house and walkway. We were careful not to harm his flower bed.

Dad made us a swing by carving out and hanging an old tire from the giant two-hundred-year-old maple that still shades the farmhouse. We would swing for hours from the tree, long hair flying in the breeze, taking turns pushing each other, patiently waiting for our turn. Occasional disagreements over whose turn it was would occur, but we resolved differences without too much fuss.

Our farm was surrounded by colorful hollyhocks that came up every year. Dad loved the beauty of the tall flowering plants that grew wild amongst the grape arbor and along the sides of the barns. He had had hollyhocks on his family farm on Bussey Road, and back in Switzerland, where his father grew up, hollyhocks were popular. When the flowers were in full bloom we made little women with full skirts using the colorful pink, red, or purple flowers for the skirts. After making a dozen or more we lined them up and imagined a formal dance!

Dandelions were plentiful in May and early June in the hayfields and in our front yard – everyone made dandelion chains. Unfortunately, they left a sticky, not easily removed mess on our hands, and even with a heavy-duty washing, the oils from the plant persisted.

Dad made us a sandbox out of an old tractor tire and filled it with concrete sand from Osborne's Construction in Elmwood. We made sure the sand stayed in the box; even though it was a cheap grade, it cost scarce money. We were happy using plastic dishes or discarded tin plates for sand toys.

My sisters, brothers, and I had fun on the farm with what was available. We swung from ropes in the hayloft or built forts in the hedgerows. We played in straw, climbed ladders, and went barefoot in the granary, even though it was off limits to us. Sometimes we snuck in and saw as many as eight or more quick-moving mice scampering from the wheat bin. I hated mice, so against my brothers' wishes I sang, stamped my feet, clapped my hands, or made strange sounds – to avoid seeing those ugly gray creatures!

Part of living on a farm was a natural inclination to get dirty. My mother was an excellent housekeeper, even with a large family, challenging environment, and limited appliances. Cow manure, hay chaff, shavings, and just plain dirt created a never-ending pile of dirty clothes. We followed the cow paths, running barefoot to the cow pasture to gather them to be milked, often stepping in freshly deposited cow poop, and then washing our feet in the stream that ran through the farm. We didn't worry about disease or infection, and never got sick.

We had a dog. (Everyone had a dog.) Our first was a collie named Sport; she had been Great-Grandma Tilden's dog. After Sport died, we had Judy, a black Lab. Judy was allowed in the house and ate out of an old plastic bowl. She never had dog food, but ate well from leftover table scraps, including cereal or a few drops of milk left from breakfast.

There were always several cats at the farm. City folks dropped cats off, thinking they would be well fed and useful taking care of the mouse population. Mom did not allow cats in the house, but Dad fed them warm milk in the barn. They also hunted field mice. After milking was done, Dad gave the cats the disposable milk filter (used to strain milk before going into the can) to lick.

Once we had a baby squirrel living in the house after its mother was killed. I faithfully got up at night and fed the squirrel warm milk from a doll bottle my friend Mary Singer loaned me. Within a few months the squirrel had to go, Mom's orders, after it climbed the curtains and scurried around the house like a rat. He was taken to the creek where other squirrels lived and released.

Summer meant a visit from Old Towl, the peddler, driving a horse and pulling a wagon full of goods. For what seemed like hours, we watched him slowly come down our country road, waiting in anticipation of some small treat given to each of us. Towl drove his horse and wagon across our front yard right up to the open porch door, mumbling from a mouth full of tobacco juice, "rags, rags, newspapers, newspapers, will trade for bleach, goods, and candy." Our mother exchanged rags and newspapers she had saved for a couple of gallons of bleach, and maybe an unusual kitchen tool. A piece of gum or small lollipop was handed to each of us, patiently waiting. We each responded with a shy smile and a quiet thank you. After a few short minutes, we watched him head west to the next house with his wagon full of wares, wondering if we would see him next year.

One week every summer Mom signed us up for Vacation Bible School at the Methodist Church in Onondaga Hill. The mornings were filled doing projects, learning Bible verses, having a snack of Kool-Aid and Oreo cookies, and then assembling with other classes to learn Christian songs and a Bible story. A Friday night program was planned and rehearsed to show off our projects and accomplishments. Mom and Dad and younger siblings always attended.

We took swimming lessons, first at Otisco Lake, later at Jamesville Beach – two weeks of lessons taking a school bus from designated spots. My siblings and I were picked up and dropped off at the corner store in South Onondaga. We packed a sandwich and purchased a treat, a plate of French Fries (my brother Hank and I shared) or a frozen Milky Way on a stick. Mort and Hank went when they were young, but were later needed on the farm.

In the evenings after supper, neighbor kids (usually the Rouse and Fellows' families) often showed up for a quick game of baseball at the open field next to our house. Dad and the boys made a makeshift backboard from old lumber and chicken wire to catch wild balls. Dad taught my brothers carpentry using materials lying around the farm. We used what was available and recycled as much

Playtime and Pets

as possible; crude bases were formed from pieces of lumber, old rug pieces or shingles. We used our creativity.

When the clotheslines were not being used we dragged pillows, bed sheets, bedspreads, and/or blankets off our beds outside and placed them over the low hanging clothesline, making a tent. Rocks collected alongside the gravel road held the tent out and kept blankets in place. Our imaginations worked as we pretended we were camping. Mom gave us permission, (after a little begging) to make peanut butter and jelly sandwiches and good old Kool-Aid – five cents a package, one cup of sugar in two quarts of water – cherry, grape, strawberry, orange or lime.

By nightfall we had the exhausting chore of removing the evidence of our pretend camping. We placed all the stones back along the ditch, every single one, bedding back on the correct beds – no need to wash it – bugs, grass, and dirt didn't bother us too much!

Saturday or Sunday afternoons during the winter, weather permitting, we sledded on our hill. After dressing with layers of clothing, sometimes socks for gloves, and oversized boots, we dragged out our two wooden sleds with steel runners that had been passed down from neighbors. After reaching the top of our enormous hill, two or three kids piled on one sled, headed down the hill picking up speed as we traveled, enjoying the brief one-minute thrill, laughing all the way. Then we had the long-tiring walk back up the steep grade, making several treks in one afternoon. Sometimes we slid down our road, not worrying about traffic – there was hardly any. The Isgar farm adjacent to our farm had great sledding opportunities, and we often went over to their hilly fields. They also had ice form at the bottom of their hill from water runoff that made for sledding on the ice. We didn't have ice skates, but made do with a cardboard box or wooden crate to slip around on.

During the winter, our barn became a haven for fun. Dad placed a regulation size basketball backboard and net in our hayloft. By early January part of the barn would be emptied out and there was space for a basketball court. On Sunday afternoons, it was a popular hangout for neighbor kids for a good old basketball game. Even though the barn was chilly, good exercise playing ball made being cold last only a short time.

Free time was filled with resourceful play. We found activities to do without money or parents entertaining us. We had the normal routines of summer, but also collected puffballs from the cow pasture, caught fireflies in the cool evenings after sunset, lay in the grass gazing at stars, played in sawdust and shavings, or made forts in the hay. Swinging from the ropes in the barn rafters, falling or dropping into piles of loose hay or straw (hitting a little hard at times) were happy times.

There were times when we had to wait or dream. Dreaming wasn't bad; Grandpa dreamed on top of Mettmenalp! We were poor in money, but rich in experience. Our family was happy and well fed, and we had a warm, loving home.

Dad and Mom taught us to improvise, making do with what

we had and taking care of it, experiencing total happiness doing so. We never felt cheated or deprived. Memories of yesteryear are of stress-free days running through fields, doing cartwheels on the lawn, laughing, being silly, using our imaginations, making believe, and taking pleasure in all the many wonderful free things surrounding our lives as farm children.

  Of course, it wasn't all apple pie and fun and games; we also had chores and responsibilities…

Playtime and Pets

Chapter 22

Expectations

Life on our farm was similar to every other – everyone had daily chores. Even though it wasn't fun, pitching in was expected. Parents had rules and kids followed them. Families were intact, divorce extremely rare. No confrontation, no complaining.

Our family of ten assembled around the kitchen table at mealtime three times a day, without exception. We enjoyed home-prepared meals that were hearty and healthy and quietly conversed and shared our day. Only pleasant, peaceful talk, without bickering, bullying, or annoying one another, was allowed.

Entitlement in our family (and most families during our mid-century period) meant the person who brought home the bacon deserved and was given respect. The chair at the head of the table belonged to my dad, and he sat there for over seventy years. We respected his place. He earned it.

Our parents believed in learning by doing. Dad used to say, "You can't drive a tractor or milk a cow by watching!" Dad learned by doing, just like his father before him. We weeded, harvested, mopped the floor, made a cake and peeled potatoes flawlessly. The more chores we did, the better we became at doing our work.

Mom and Dad also believed we learned by our mistakes. One time they went out to dinner to celebrate their anniversary, and using ingredients on hand, I made a special two-tiered cake. The second tier was pink, using red food coloring, but I forgot to add baking powder to the second batch. Needless to say, the pink tier was flat and heavy. I only made that mistake once. My family got a good laugh out of my attempt to make a special cake for our parents.

Everyone in the family was up by eight. My brothers Hank and Mort had to be up earlier to help with chores and milk the cows. If they overslept, Dad would hit two galvanized milk can covers together until there was some movement at the house. Sometimes I buried my head in the pillow to block out the loud clanging. I am sure it could be heard for miles.

Dad was not happy if he came in from the barn for breakfast and found anyone in bed. He was the authority and our boundaries were clear: work had to be done and early mornings were the best time to get moving. Every day for breakfast we had white toast, homemade strawberry or blackberry jam, a bowl of cereal with rich Jersey milk, and a small four-ounce glass of orange juice. (No more – orange juice was a costly commodity and was served for good health, our daily vitamin C.)

Because seniority had its privileges, as soon as everyone else left the table my sisters closest to me in age (Karen and Beverly) and I would hand wash and dry all the dishes, then sweep the spacious kitchen floor. We didn't need to be told. We weren't given allowances. We never sat around until our favorite television program was over. Mealtime chores were repeated three times a day without whining or moaning. If we hesitated we knew we would get it. (I never knew what we would get, but I knew it was something I didn't want!)

    Laundry day wasn't just Monday – with our large family and limited clothing, it was done most days except Sunday. Before an automatic washer and dryer we used a wringer washer. Clothes were fed individually into the wringer and dropped from there into the rinse water in our claw-footed, free-standing tub, and then went once more through the wringer. Mom warned us about the danger of getting an arm or hand caught in the wringer. Our parents taught us to respect machinery as they had learned from their parents. I helped Mom hang wet clothes on the line attached from one maple tree to another which filled most of the front lawn. We hung cloth handkerchiefs, shirts by the tails, and socks by the toes, using wooden clothespins. Diapers filled at least one string of clothesline and later in the day I took them down. (During winter months stiff, frozen diapers were brought in from outside and draped over a folding clothes rack near the register in the dining room to finish the drying.) All the clothes were folded on our large dining room table and put away immediately, another rule of Mom's.

    Our large vegetable garden was located at different times behind the house, the side of the house or across the road and needed daily attention. Location varied and crops were rotated to keep soil from being depleted of valuable nutrients, smart farming techniques which insured good product yield. Mornings during hot summer months were the best time to pull weeds, and sometimes we struggled with the tough deep-rooted weeds, pulling so hard we fell on our butts! Dad was an expert gardener, having learned from childhood how to grow and sell produce. He stressed the importance of weeding – if you were old enough to know a weed from a plant, you were in the garden helping out. When vegetables were mature, we harvested them for eating, canning, or freezing.

Our big meal was at noon, and vegetables from the garden were the central part. Peas served in small bowls with milk and butter, green and yellow beans, spinach, Swiss chard, new potatoes (sometimes called salt potatoes because of the size), were on the menu. Picking and shelling peas was the most tedious job. Bending over or sliding on our behinds in the hot, humid morning sun gathering vegetables seemed endless. After harvesting we sat under the shade of the maple tree in our front yard and shelled peas or "head and tailed" the beans. Often we ate enough raw vegetables to fill our daily requirement of vitamins and minerals! Mom didn't care because we had a surplus of garden vegetables, but she cautioned us not to eat too many and get a bellyache or diarrhea. When it was time to can or freeze, Karen and Beverly helped and the younger girls, Shirley and Christine, would attempt to pick. (I was almost sixteen when our youngest sibling, Heidi was born.) Some days we picked several baskets of produce and spent the afternoon in the hot kitchen, either blanching the vegetables for freezing or filling quart jars and placing them, seven at a time, in the canner on the stove, creating heavy steam in the already hot day of summer. In early fall, we canned Bartlett pears and Seckel pears from our trees and bought a bushel of peaches to can also. The shelves in the cellarway were soon loaded with jars of corn, beans, tomatoes, fruit, and bread and butter pickles from our summer of canning, helping with food costs and winter enjoyment.

    My two brothers, Hank and Mort, had endless responsibilities every day, working side by side with Dad harvesting wheat, oats, or corn and baling hay, neatly stacking bales in the hayloft during hot, humid summer days, in addition to milking cows morning and night. Weather dictated the length of the haying season – too much rain, not enough rain (a series of hot dry days was needed) – farmers were at the mercy of the weather. The boys had to clean barns (before automatic barn cleaners), fix fences, and spread manure in the fields.

    Every spring after plowing, a new crop of stones appeared in the fields. Before planting, the exhausting job of "picking stones" had to be completed. Dad used a stone boat (a crude 8 foot by 4-foot flat raft of wood bolted together front and back) with a large steel loop hooked to the front with chains to attach to the tractor so the tractor could drag it. Dad drove the tractor with the stone boat attached throughout the field, stopping frequently along the way to pick up rocks. Several family members might tag along to help, but

Expectations

lifting heavy stones was saved for our muscular Dad or brothers. When the stone boat could hold no more it was dragged to the edge of the field or hedgerow and manually unloaded.

Mom had a "thing" about girls working in the barn and fields. Once in a while we drove the tractor, milked cows, fed the young stock, or helped load or unload hay, but only when there was too much for my brothers and Dad to do or we needed to get hay in the barn before rain. We did gather cows from the hill when a simple "caboss" call would not work. Most of the time cows were waiting at the gate across the road from the milking parlor eager to have their swollen bags relieved of the pressure of their milk. Traffic stopped on our little-traveled road and people in cars waited patiently until the cows crossed.

In addition to daily chores, every summer we completed specific jobs. Mom's daily goal was to stay ahead of the housework, cleaning, and cooking. Dresser drawers and closets were cleaned and clothes sorted, bags of clothes only good for rags were put aside for our summer visit from old Towl, the ragman. Summer was the time to wallpaper at least one of our six bedrooms. Mom selected pretty floral designs or appropriate designs for my brothers' room, and ordered through mail order companies specializing in wallpaper and borders. We even had to wallpaper the ceiling in a contrasting off-white design. Wallpapering was a job I dreaded, as patience wore thin for everyone. In the heat of summer, little ones created havoc by getting into paste or stepping on recycled newspaper placed on the floor to protect wallpaper strips to be pasted. No self-sticking wallpaper or fancy gadgets were available during the fifties.

Even if we had money we were taught to make do and improvise with what we had around the house. Money was stretched to purchase bare necessities, not on seldom used tools or gimmicks. We purchased needs, not wants. We recycled everything: plastic bowls for the dog's dishes, bailing twine to tie calves in their pens, fabric from colorful feed bags for clothes, an old tractor tire for a makeshift sand box, or a smaller tire for a swing.

Getting dirty, sweaty, sunburned, and weary from endless chores was part of living on a farm. We never thought of work as being difficult, never felt a sense of being poor. We were always grateful for meager babysitting money or second-hand clothing, and wonderful Christmases with plenty for all. Excitement and dreams filled our days and nights.

A large six-bedroom house to keep clean, eight kids, endless dirty laundry, cooking three substantial meals, all without a dishwasher, automatic washing machine or dryer demanded lots of planning and organization. Our parents taught us to work together as a team; sharing the workload was quicker and more efficient. They depended on every one of us to pitch in and help. This became even more crucial when Mom started working away from home.

Expectations

Chapter 23

Mom's New Job

Mom was a typical stay-at-home mom adhering to the nonverbal requirements expected of mothers in the 1950's. She didn't learn to drive until then; many women never learned to drive as they didn't feel the necessity with one-car families and stores that closed nightly at 6 p.m., noon on Saturday and closed Sunday. Often men stopped on the way home from work and bought groceries. The majority of Mom's shopping was done using Sears or Montgomery Ward catalogs. She cooked, grocery shopped with my father, washed, ironed, and cleaned but hated to sew. Dad was at our simple Singer sewing machine mending his torn work pants when needed. Mom completed all the obligations of running the house of ten lovingly (or, at least, pretended to) without complaint.

When I was about ten, Mom jumped at an opportunity to be a home demonstrator for Tupperware – a new concept of home parties. Parties were held in the evening after dinner was over and the younger children dressed for bed – a perfect time. Bravely, Mom drove all over Onondaga County including Syracuse to hold her parties. She had to get clear directions – GPS or last minute cell phone directions were not available. Once or twice she was stood up (lights out, no one home) when she arrived at her destination. She carried two large green suitcases packed efficiently so all samples neatly fit, and off we would go, me wearing a dress, nice white socks, and tied shoes. What a treat to have Mom to myself as this rarely happened!

Even though I was quite young, I was a big help as well as company for Mom. I passed out sales booklets, order sheets, and pencils, and quietly sat near the demonstration table. Part of Mom's demonstration was to throw a sealed bowl of water in the air and let it fall to the floor; this always brought gasps and laughs from her guests. Never once did the bowl come unsealed. The hostess served a yummy dessert to her guests. Mom and I graciously accepted and enjoyed this part of the evening. While she was adding up her sales I packed her suitcases, saving us some time. Occasionally she would be thrilled: she had big sales and more bookings – and these kept her home-party business going.

About a year later Mom started selling Sarah Coventry jewelry. Same arrangement – I went with her, but it was less work setting up. She carried one medium suitcase, brought a large black felt cloth that went on the table first, and a raised shelf to display the sparkling necklaces and earrings. The earrings sold were clip type only, as not many women had pierced ears in the 1950's. Special individual time spent with my mom made me feel important and grown up.

Mom's New Job

Schedules changed quickly when I was twelve. Mom was offered a job bagging apples at Beak and Skiff Apple Orchards. Dad said she could work only if Grandma Tilden watched my youngest sisters, Shirley and Christine, who were not yet in school. Mom drove up the hill and asked her mother if she would be interested. Grandma Tilden was a widow at forty-five, had very limited resources, and did not drive. Babysitting appeared to be an ideal job and would help both my parents and Grandma out financially.

Mom's new job was seasonal, mid-August to March. She worked standing on her feet from 7 a.m. to 4:15 p.m. in a cold storage barn with two fifteen-minute coffee breaks and a half-hour lunch. The rest of the time she stood sorting and bagging apples, lifting and tugging all day long, not an easy job.

Soon my own routine changed considerably. At twelve, I had to get up before Mom left for work and make five lunches for my sisters and brothers. We didn't have a lot of sandwich choices, just peanut butter and jelly or jam, egg salad, or bologna. I spread the bread out on the counter using almost a whole loaf, making them assembly-line fashion. (My brother Mort wanted one peanut butter sandwich and one jam sandwich – not mixed – and I had to clean the knife before cutting into the other.) I wrapped each sandwich in waxed paper, along with one of Grandma's Tilden's homemade cookies, and a crisp apple from the three-pound bag Mom brought home daily. These were placed in brown paper bags with initials written on the outside and included three cents twisted in wax paper for milk. Pennies tied in a handkerchief were placed in the tin lunch pails the younger kids carried. Days that Dad worked on construction I also made a lunch for him, a healthy sandwich of meat and cheese. He had to be out the door before the school bus came.

After lunches were made, I checked that everyone was up. The boys were in the barn doing chores and the girls needed to be out of the only bathroom before they came in to shower and get ready for school. I set the table with cereal bowls and small glasses for orange juice, and everyone fended for themselves. Another unwritten rule was that we all had to eat breakfast, at least cereal (sometimes I made oatmeal or Ralston), milk, and orange juice. Toast was optional. We never had pop tarts, donuts, snack food or soda for breakfast!

Mom came home from work exhausted and chilled to the bone, and warmed up sitting in a chair next to the heat register in the center of our dining room. To keep ahead of the massive amount of laundry, she routinely placed a load of dirty clothes in the washer, then the dryer, and finally lay down.

Before I started supper, I would peek in and quietly ask Mom what to make for dinner if she hadn't already told me. Sometimes she gave me several suggestions and I would decide, but she always had an idea of what was going to be prepared for dinner and had meat thawing before she left for work in the morning. Occasionally there would be a pot roast simmering that Grandma Tilden started around three. I knew without instructions from Mom to peel potatoes and carrots and add to the kettle for dinner. After the vegetables were cooked I made gravy from the broth in the pot. The old standby was potatoes, eaten most days of the week. In the cellar was an enormous pile of potatoes in a crudely made bin on the dirt floor. Nightly I had to go down the narrow, rickety stairway (which lacked a railing) to the cellar. I peeled the potatoes, planning the cooking time, so they were ready for 6:30 dinner, when my dad and brothers came in to eat. By spring the potatoes began to shrivel and the wrinkled skin made peeling difficult. The sprouting potatoes were used for seed by cutting them into quarters, making sure each section had an eye. Dad put them in water overnight and then planted them the next day after the ground was frost free – another frugal attempt to aid family finances!

If ground beef was thawing I might make a meatloaf with baked potatoes, or goulash, or Spanish rice with canned tomatoes from our fifty to seventy quarts preserved from our garden, or hamburger patties, or hamburger gravy. (Hamburger is versatile!) Mashed potatoes and steak were prepared quite often as we had our own beef. My least favorite was Mom's homemade vegetable beef soup, for when we were down to cooking soup bones; we knew another cow soon had to be sent to the slaughterhouse. Chicken was reserved for Sunday, killed and cleaned on Saturday for the Sunday meal.

When Mom got up from her much needed power nap, she sorted the dried clothes into piles on the dining room table and each of us was told to immediately take them to our rooms and put them away – a rule she enforced. Her dining room table held only a centerpiece.

Having Grandma Tilden come to our house each day and care for the preschool kids was a blessing. If she had refused to take care of my sisters, Mom could not have worked outside the home. There were no daycare facilities, only grandmas and other stay-at-home moms willing to babysit. Grandma had no workplace skills, and never drove, but conveniently lived just up the hill from our house. Dad picked her up just before the school bus arrived. She welcomed the extra money, ten to fifteen dollars a week taken from the seventy or eighty dollars Mom brought home. Dad was around but had farm work to do and sometimes he worked on construction from 8 a.m. to 4 p.m. and then came home to farm chores and milking.

Grandma was a life saver for Mom. Not only did she babysit, she ironed for hours every Monday – cotton blouses, skirts, pants, shirts (no permanent-press clothes were available then). On Fridays before the grocery shopping, Grandma cleaned out the refrigerator and defrosted the freezer section. Every day she swept, sometimes mopped, and vacuumed, besides watching the little ones. Grandma also baked cookies every day! We looked forward to seeing the round Tupperware container filled, especially with Grandma's soft chocolate cookies made with sour milk. She made her own homemade sour milk, using a little cider vinegar in our rich

Jersey milk, and allowing the milk to sour for one hour. Nine cookies were discreetly saved for dinner and seven for our lunches, including Mom's.

Grandma Tilden's Chocolate Cookies

Friday was payday. Grandma and Mom went to the A&P supermarket at the Valley Plaza and sometimes stopped at Kresge's 5 & 10 cent store next door. Usually only one or two kids went along, and whoever went was allowed to pick out one bag of candy (29 cents) to pass out later that night everyone getting the same amount. Sharing was part of learning as children.

Saturday mornings we watched Sky King, Roy Rogers, and the Lone Ranger after our individual chores were done. My job every Saturday was to make one or two apple pies and an additional crust or graham cracker pie for Sunday dinner. Skills like this, taught to me as early as ten, are forever etched in my memory.

With Mom's new job I was exposed to adult responsibilities and maturity. It helped me become more unselfish (so many people to care for) and conscientious. I had to be dependable – much was expected of me. There were no days off, and we had to persevere, even when sick or hurt.

Chapter 24

Doctor Visits

As children we seldom saw doctors; cuts and bruises were taken in stride. We were taught to tough it out unless seriously injured or very sick. Our parents did not have medical insurance or Medicaid. We received required shots at school with the rest of the class, lining up in a row and dreading the needle. One such shot was the polio vaccination, stemming the fear of the raging epidemic striking many young people in the 1950's.

Farm injuries were easy to come by, and each one of my seven siblings had injuries. Once a pitchfork punctured the top of my foot when I tripped and the fork bounced back. Soaking the foot in hot water with a little salt was my first treatment, but two or three days later a noticeable large, red, swollen area appeared on the top of my foot. A trip to the doctor, a shot of penicillin, and white pills to take until they were all gone did the job of healing.

Bike injuries were common on our gravel road. Once I chipped one of my front teeth falling off my bike, experienced weeks of severe mouth pain, and then saw a specialist for root canal surgery, traumatic fifty or sixty years ago. Novocain froze the area and a cut was made on the gum above the injured tooth, causing blood to trickle down my throat causing me to gag as the assistant suctioned blood from my mouth. After the lengthy procedure, the doctor sewed up the incision with black thread. My tooth turned light gray, an unsightly reminder throughout high school and college. After working a few years and acquiring dental insurance, I finally had the tooth capped.

Another time I fell off my bike racing down our steep hill. I injured my left arm and suffered with pain and could not use the arm for a few days before my parents sought medical help. They took me to see a family friend, Dr. Van Lengen at People's Hospital, an oversized house on Delaware Street. When the doctor touched my arm, I yelled. I had a broken left wrist. A nurse with a crisp, white uniform and cap had me lay on a small narrow table where the doctor and nurse set my arm using long pieces of white meshed cotton dipped in a milky solution, wrapping them around my arm – a messy plaster of Paris. The cast was on my left wrist for eight weeks.

My next hospital visit was a five-day stay while I was a cheerleader in high school. Cheerleading in the 1960's was a big deal – girls couldn't participate in sports (or compete with other schools like the boys) until after a law was passed in 1972. Title IX – Education Amendment Act gave girls and boys equitable opportunities to participate in sports and appropriate funding.

My older brother Hank was named lineman of the week for

Doctor Visits

football and attended states for wrestling. My younger brother Don, (nicknamed Mort) was outstanding in football and was the leading scorer in the Onondaga County Southern Division basketball for two seasons. Mort was a great shooter from outside and short enough, at five foot nine, to draw the fouls and made many of those shots from the line. He was in the 1000-point club before three-point shots were made a basketball regulation. My brothers' athletic talents inspired me to play sports, but my only opportunity to show my athletic ability was cheerleading. Unfortunately, it was short-lived. During practice, just after the New Year, in the heart of basketball season, I landed hard and twisted my knee during practice. Limping around in severe pain, I still cheered. I was not going to give up my only athletic showcase. The cheerleading squad willingly changed cheers so I wasn't required to jump. After games, I went home and soaked in a tub of very hot water, sobbing with pain. No health provider or coach told me icing the injury was better treatment. Finally, during the fall of the following year, I saw a specialist. A vial of yellow fluid was removed from my knee and the doctor said I needed surgery for a torn cartilage. There was no MRI or CT scan to confirm this; it was just an educated guess. High-tech, specialized medical imaging was not available for another decade.

   Surgery was scheduled for Thursday, November 9, 1962, at St. Joseph's Hospital in Syracuse. Mom and Dad were not able to visit much, as I had an eight-month-old sister, Heidi, at home. Mom worked at Beak and Skiff and Dad had the dairy farm and outside carpentry work and they weren't given paid personal days from their jobs. I was left alone, in unbearable pain most of the time, in a ward with five other women. One nurse told me to stop moaning or they'd place me in a different room. One friendly patient spoke up and said, "No, we want her here with us!"

After three days of misery I wanted out. I was given crutches and then allowed to go home since I couldn't eat or sleep. After two weeks at home I was looking forward to going back to school, even though I could hardly sleep or eat, and lost thirteen pounds. I hobbled around school on crutches with a blood-soaked bandage, struggling to catch up on school work. We had no tutors or extra help then – if you missed school for any length of time it was your responsibility to get the work and complete assignments.

Dad seldom got sick and did not complain. His illnesses were treated with home remedies, but he knew at what point he had to go to a doctor. Unplanned accidents and illness occur in everyone's life; Dad was no exception and had a farm accident in 1958. While backing up carrying a stone boat with my brother Hank on one end, he fell backwards down an open hay hole to the concrete floor below. With Dad's dead weight, my brother struggled with all his strength to get Dad to the house and to the bedroom with one arm under his shoulder. After a short time lying on the bed, Mom decided to call an ambulance. We had no local emergency facilities with trained personnel then. It seemed like hours before the ambulance from downtown Syracuse pulled into our driveway!

Doctor Visits

While the medical staff placed Dad in the ambulance, the school bus driver was driving by as he was finishing his 5:00 run. He parked the 60-passenger school bus in the barnyard so he could help my fifteen-year-old brother milk the cows. (Farmers relied on the neighbors in times of illness, tragedy or death. People brought food and helped with chores.)

Dad spent a few days in the hospital with a mild concussion and dislocated shoulder, but swiftly went back to work on the farm. We had no insurance or medical assistance – his recuperation therapy was getting back to the barn! Payments to the doctor and hospital were made each month faithfully; Mom added this unplanned expense to her list of never-ending bills.

Dad suffered a ruptured appendix in October 1964. At that time surgery of any kind was not easy. After a five-day stay in the hospital, he recuperated at home before going back to the farm and milking cows. Cows had to be milked. My brothers Hank and Mort, and Bill Kelsey, a neighbor boy, were old enough to pick up the slack. Again, Dad was in the barn working sooner than he should have been, lifting and tugging doing daily chores.

We saw Dr. Burak when there was a need. Most times he worked alone or had his wife assist as receptionist/nurse. Our visits were infrequent – infections and colds seemed to take care of themselves. Once I had bronchitis during the summer and stayed in bed using Vicks. After several days of trying home remedies I saw Dr. Burak, who gave me a shot of penicillin and small white packet of pills with instructions to take them until they were gone. Seldom was there a need to go to a drug store for a prescription.

My brother Mort had ringworm (a fungal disease in a ring-shaped patch) on his scalp which he caught from the cows. Some of us girls had it on our arms or legs. We received purple salve from the doctor, rubbed it in, and wrapped it up with strips of torn white sheets to prevent spreading. We didn't see a specialist, and we didn't tell our friends.

While Mort's ringworm was healing, he was tossing a baseball off the roof of the shed at the end of the driveway and the hard ball hit his head precisely where the tender scalp was healing. Blood spurted out quickly, and he ran to the house, pressing his head, trying to stop the bleeding. Mom frantically called the doctor for advice, but he only said, "Can't do anything about it, can't put a tourniquet around his neck." He then chastised her for allowing an eleven-year-old boy to play with a ball with his serious skin condition. After many agonizing moments, the bleeding stopped without emergency room or medical intervention. Mort's healing was only delayed.

In January 1952 when my sister Beverly was only six weeks old, Dr. Gak, our country doctor made a house call. Hank, Mort, Karen and I sat on the couch in the living room, stiff as statues, wide-eyed, staring at the doctor while he examined her. She lay naked on the dining room table, kicking and weakly crying. After diagnosing her with pneumonia, her treatment was a shot of penicillin. Mom, upset by her diagnosis, drove up the hill to her mother's house crying after the doctor left. Pneumonia was a very scary illness at such a young age.

Every summer my brothers and sisters and I saw the dentist for yearly checkups. (We would single out any sibling who had a cavity and give them a little jab about their misfortune.) Our dentist, Dr. Burke, did everything in the office. He had a small waiting room upstairs in a house with a private entrance, and an office with desk, phone and appointment book. He pulled teeth, filled cavities, and cleaned teeth with no assistant or receptionist.

I needed braces and was sent to an orthodontist. Four permanent teeth had to be removed to make room to straighten teeth in my small mouth. Dr. Burke pulled them in his office with Novocain, two at a time. The monthly payment for the braces was twenty-five dollars, a lot of money. Yearly dental checkups were a costly commodity. My parents sacrificed so I could have a healthy mouth and retain a pleasant smile. Throughout the years I have been blessed and I'm still grateful for their generosity.

Visiting doctors was only after home remedies didn't work. Most farm families learned from their parents, who in turn had learned from their parents, what to do for illness or injuries. Nutmeg and lard smeared on a cloth was pinned on nightwear for a cold. Watkins' ointment was an old standby for cuts, scrapes and bites. Baking soda and warm water was used for indigestion or as toothpaste. Sunburns were treated with vinegar and water or aloe.

We did well with what we had.

I knew no one, adult or child, taking medication for anxiety, insomnia, hypertension, or allergies! We ate peanut butter for lunch, not fearing allergic reactions. We went to a doctor to receive a shot of penicillin or small package of pills. If you needed stitches they were done in the office. There were no large pharmacies at every corner. No one took numerous prescriptions or had plastic pill boxes on the kitchen table. Medically it was a different world.

Our animals also required health care...

Chapter 25

Treating Sick Cows and Calves

Unplanned, hefty expenses occurred quite often on our farm – machinery breaking down, flat tires, gas stolen from the farm fuel tank, and sickness were just a few. But one of the most devastating costs was the death of a sick cow or calf before the vet made it to our farm. Loss of these animals painfully affected bottom line profits.

I have vivid memories of a cow lying on her side in the pasture, unable to get up and Dad's urgency summoning the family veterinarian, Dr. John Stack. Frequently an older cow (usually one of our best milk producers) that had just had a calf got milk fever. Milk fever is a metabolic disease caused by a low blood calcium level. If not treated with a calcium injection intravenously, death is imminent.

Dr. Stack arrived quickly after a phone call. After locating Dad in the pasture, the vet drove his car to the site, got out wearing his rubber boots, opened the trunk, and pulled out necessary medical supplies. A large needle attached to a long hose and bottle of life-saving medicine (calcium) was inserted in the cow's neck. Within minutes she perked up, lifted her limp head, struggled to get up, and with a little tugging from Dad, was up on all four legs. After the amazing recovery, Dr. Stack added five dollars to Dad's bill and left until the next emergency. (Decades later farmers were trained to administer some medicines and drugs to sick animals without the vet; a refrigerator in the barn solely to hold medicine would become common. Better care of the cow before and after delivery, such as a special diet, also lowered the chance of cows getting milk fever.)

In the early 1950's we had a cow quarantined with the possibility of rabies. She was tied up in a pen, far from the rest of the herd, foaming from the mouth with scary bulging eyes, while Dad waited for her to die (she had to die on her own to get a proper diagnosis). Dad warned us sternly to stay away from her. After she died her head was transferred to Cornell for a brain biopsy to confirm the vet's suspicions. The cow was rabid, and her body was destroyed. We had news media at the farm for a local television broadcast about the cow, warning people about rabid foxes attacking herds and pets, creating fear of an epidemic in the area.

Mastitis is a serious illness cows occasionally acquire after giving birth – inflammation of the cow's udder, usually the result of a bacterial infection. Dad would sometimes see swelling and redness in the mammary gland, quickly diagnose the infection, and treat it with penicillin. But the cow's milk could not be used until after the penicillin was out of the cow's system. Periodically, milk plants tested milk and if they found evidence of penicillin, farmers could be fined, or worse, be unable to ship any milk. Dad was careful to dump cow's milk treated with an antibiotic; besides the vet bill, loss of milk resulted in another blow to revenue.

Another serious illness that caused financial hardship and sometimes resulted in death without treatment was diarrhea in calves, usually ones a few weeks old. Dad was aware that calves were susceptible to diarrhea, and recognized it quickly so appropriate treatment could be made. He checked the eyeballs to see if they had sunken in, and sometimes pinched the skin over the neck and gave it a twist to see if it snapped back normally or returned too slowly. If calves were at an early stage of diarrhea he treated them with fluids (oral electrolytes – calcium, bicarbonates, sodium and potassium), but if the calf did not respond to oral therapy, or was too sick to drink or suck, Dad had to call the vet for intravenous fluids and antibiotics.

Ringworm (tinea), a very contagious skin disease due to a fungus, infected some cows and calves. It was contracted from soil which contained the fungus. Unfortunately, if not treated it would quickly spread to other animals or even to us. The vet would supply Dad with a salve to cure this unsightly skin infection before it spread.

Another danger was unexpected summer thunder and lightning storms that could potentially strike and kill a cow sheltering under one of our weeping willows along the creek bed. These brutal summer storms put Dad on edge; once we lost two cows instantly when lightning struck a tree, splitting it in half and electrically killing the cows standing under the tree. One nearby farmer lost three cows drinking at a watering trough – the lightning hit a wire attached to the trough and fused the cows' bones while they were still standing. The farmer found them still standing next to the trough dead – he gave them a little nudge and they fell over in a heap.

    Another unplanned threat to our herd was hardware disease, which occurred when a simple wire or nail penetrated the lining of the gut causing infection. Sometimes cows ate hay or silage that contained old wire or nails which had been ground up in the chopper or baler and then ended up in the feeding trough. Grazing cows also might eat old fence wire lying in the fields. Cows first showed signs of having hardware when they were "off feed," as Dad would say. They experienced abdominal pain and would not eat, extending the head and neck, and this often proved fatal. Treatment was difficult, and usually Dad sent the cow to the slaughterhouse to be butchered for family food – another loss of milk production and smaller milk check. As years passed, farmers sometimes forced a magnet down the throats of young stock. The magnets stayed in the first stomach, attracting any nails or wires that found their way into their food. Some farm equipment now has magnets built in to collect unwanted wire. Because of hardware disease, many farmers have discontinued using wire on their bales, replacing it with twine or string. (Once while visiting Grandpa Luchsinger on his farm, he rubbed his arm against one of his cows and was pricked! After investigating, he

Treating Sick Cows and Calves

found a wire was poking out of the cow's side, and he pulled out a piece of old fence wire. The cow miraculously survived.)

Unforeseen sickness and the death of animals left Dad wondering what would be next, but he readily moved on, knowing he had no control of the unexpected. He went forward with a positive attitude, working long hours every day to pay for unplanned expenses, and supplementing income whenever he could. Often, we benefited from Dad's skill at hunting; hunting put food on the table and also eliminated unwanted pests – and it was fun!

Happy Cows

Treating Sick Cows and Calves

Chapter 26

Hunting

Dad loved to hunt! He hunted for the sport, money, and meat. He had his gun and his green hunting jacket ready at a moment's notice to hunt raccoon, deer, pheasants, woodchucks, and rats – anything that was good eating or a nuisance. Dad called the raccoons "masked bandits" because they robbed a field of corn at night, stripping the stalks just before harvest resulting in our wonderful field of sweet corn gone! Raccoons made a mess and did considerable damage around the farm, attracted by abundant food, refuge in barns or storage sheds, and plenty of water. The best way to solve the problem was coon hunts.

First Dad scouted the area near the farm looking for a raccoon's hangout, usually a hollow tree, a corner in the barn, in the woods, on Chapman's land on Bussey Road, or even in the silo. It didn't take Dad long to find a favorite habitat after finding evidence, such as footprints, feces, or chewed up corn cobs. After dark, he went back to the den prepared for the kill, wearing high rubber boots, carrying a flashlight, handmade wooden club, and his 22 rifle. Making a little ruckus, swinging the club and pounding the tree, Dad flushed the coons out; most weighted thirty to forty pounds. He didn't have coon dogs as many hunters did, but occasionally took his brother-in-law Herb (age 12 or 13 at the time). Once Dad shot a forty-pound coon that crawled deep in the hollow of a tree, but he couldn't retrieve it. Making sure the coon was dead by poking it with the end of his rifle or his club, he lowered Herb head first, down the hole, holding onto his ankles, and slowly lifted him back up, Herb holding the heavy raccoon. As years passed, Dad took my brother Mort along with him to retrieve coons from the hollow trees.

Processing dead coons for their skins took some time. Dad hung them upside down by the back feet in the old milk house and carefully skinned them with his sharp hunting knife, making sure not to ruin the tails. The skins were stretched and dried on boards lined up along the wall until he had enough to sell to a fur dealer. Dad received two dollars for each pelt. He got rid of a nuisance, had a little fun, and made a little cash!

Hunting deer was a sport my dad, brothers, uncles, and cousins all loved. In the forties and fifties, the deer population in our area was slim; however, the Northern Tier had plenty of deer, and he looked forward to yearly hunting trips in the north woods. After making sure he had coverage for farm chores, Dad ventured out for several days (or sometimes just a day) with his brother John in Boonville. We heard many stories about the ones that got away, their kill being stolen, jammed guns, or missed shots. As the years passed, Dad hunted around central New York as deer flourished due to fewer hunters and plenty of corn, soy, and hay. Dad did not need a hunting license to hunt on his own land.

From one of Dad's many successful hunts

More times than not, Dad brought home a nice big buck and hung it by its rack from one of the maple trees in the front yard for a few days before having the meat cut up for our freezer. Most of my sisters and I never acquired a taste for venison, even when Mom made Swiss steak, or fried it with lots of butter and garlic salt.

Sometimes Dad disguised the deer meat by making homemade sauerbraten but I always knew it was venison.

A few prize deer heads were proudly mounted and hung in our living room, Dad placing his guns on the antlers as part of our living room décor! Hunting deer eliminated a nuisance, made good eating for the family, provided enjoyment of hunting, and a change in routine from the daily workload.

Pheasants, with their bright red feathers, were a favorite prey every fall around the farm. Dad scouted them out on the tractor, locating where they bedded down for the night. He learned early morning was the best time to hunt pheasants while they were in the grass looking for food, or early in the evening before bedding down for the night. During pheasant season the killed birds would be stashed in the stairway of the outside entrance to the cellar. After school, my brother Hank would run to see how many were shot; there was a limit of two each day and most often Dad shot the limit. Pheasants were good eating especially the plump breast meat, but we had to be careful we didn't bite into a pellet – using a number 5 lead shot meant lots of pellets in the bird. Unfortunately, the sport of hunting pheasant vanished as the birds have all but disappeared from loss of habitat. Now there are only rare sightings of these beautiful birds.

There was lots of target practice on the farm. Guns were placed in the rafters in the barn, by the milk house door, in the entranceway to the kitchen and on the deer antlers. When opportunity arose, guns were easy to grab. It was not unusual to hear gunshots anytime, sometimes from a distance when a woodchuck (another nuisance on the farm) might pop his head out of a hole on the hillside which turned into a good target. Pigeons, crows, squirrels, and rabbits were all fair game, providing lots of shooting for Dad and my brothers. But shooting rats brought the greatest satisfaction to the family – no one liked rats, and on any farm there were rats. They moved into the warmth of the barn where there was abundant food – corn, oats, and wheat, and crawled along the beams above the cows, waiting for night to make their move to eat. Stray cats and our dog Judy helped reduce the rat population, but a few shots with a 22 also got rid of them.

    Rats also congregated in our cellar, especially after cold weather arrived. They loved to hang out around the bottom of the coal burning furnace and later our oil furnace. It had an enclosed section where the heat rose from the cellar to the first floor register and around this heat source was an outer airspace. From the register in the dining room, using a flashlight and gun, Dad or my brothers aimed precisely at the eyes, eliminating the rat and then went to the cellar and removed the dead carcass.

    Rats and mice also hung out in the corn cribs, but with careful planning, shooting them was easy. The hunter had to be ready, and when a few ears of corn were removed, they tried to scurry away. Dad warned my brothers not shoot at the tin roof causing leakage resulting in spoiled corn and reminded them to

Hunting

remove all the dead rodents from the corn crib. Years later grandsons loved to hunt in the corncribs but was given the same stern warnings from Dad.

We had hunting traditions. Besides Dad's annual trips north, Uncle John and Aunt Ruth came to our house on Thanksgiving Eve and stayed overnight. Early Thanksgiving morning, anyone who wanted to hunt deer was welcome to go; the trucks left by 6 a.m., for the Lafayette area. Mom, my sisters, and I helped prepare a huge turkey dinner with all the trimmings along with an assortment of pies. When the men arrived back home we were eager to see if they hung a deer or two from the trees out front. (Guns were lined up on the porch, but no one went near them, a lesson we learned as early as we could understand "Don't Touch!") Hunting was thus a social as well as practical event. People worked together for a common goal. It was an important part of our limited social calendar – like all farm families, our free time was as scarce as our money!

Chapter 27

Social Calendar

Mom and Dad didn't experience social lives as we know them today. Their lives were centered on work, church, family, school, and neighbors. They focused on day-to-day needs of the family farm. Mom didn't have time to attend the Ladies Aid Society or church circles, nor did she have time to become a Girl Scout or 4-H leader or Sunday school teacher; however, my sisters and I all participated in many activities.

Household skills were reinforced through 4-H clubs, with emphasis on sewing, cooking, baking, home decorating, gardening, canning and nutrition. My 4-H leader Helen Fisher taught me how to sew, helping select appropriate patterns and fabrics to make jumpers, skirts and blouses. (This was one skill not learned at home – Mom hated to sew.) My brothers and I also exhibited our Jersey calves at the County 4-H Fair and Parish Show near Auburn a few times.

Girls Scouts was a big part of my sisters' and my outside interests and activities. Evelyn Brown added to my skills in sewing. After work Mom picked me up at her house, waiting patiently in the car while I finished. Elinor Hitchings, another Girl Scout Leader, was instrumental in my aspiration to attend college. During our junior year she facilitated trips for our troop to visit several colleges and motivated me to go, and I am forever grateful for her insight and planting the seed for my future. I was involved in scouting until I graduated from high school and was selected from Onondaga County to attend the 1962 Girl Scout National Roundup in Burlington, Vermont. Four weekends of training took place at Camp Hoover near Tully, NY during the spring in preparation for the two-week affair held in July. (Setting up two-man tents, cooking over a fire, and building fires were part of this training.) At this very same time Mom was expecting a baby (number eight!), but amiably encouraged me to attend and have the experience of a lifetime. Sister Heidi was born just after I returned home from one of those weekends (May 20, 1962).

In the early seventies Mom and Dad served on church committees. Dad had a three-year term as an elder and was chairman of Building and Grounds. He reluctantly attended monthly meetings sometimes lasting until midnight; his mindset was always to get a problem fixed or repaired immediately instead of waiting for approval. He often fixed or repaired the problem instead of hiring someone, not understanding the need to go through proper channels first. Mom served three-year terms as deacon several times, taking her to the sick, elderly, and shut-ins – a perfect post for her as she had a gift for nurturing. She prepared and served communion and

Social Calendar

was on other committees and projects delegated to the deacons.

My brothers played on Little League baseball and basketball teams. Games were held evenings during the week or Saturday mornings, but never on Sunday – Sunday was reserved for family and church. However, for a brief time our church, along with other churches on Onondaga Hill, had a Sunday night basketball league. My brother Hank played on the church team. Mort played on Little League basketball teams, once going to New York City to play in a tournament.

We attended Sunday school every Sunday without fail. My sisters, brothers, and I received our own Bibles on Children's Day when we each reached fourth grade and were able to recite the Lord's Prayer, Apostles' Creed, 23rd Psalm, and John 3:16. At the end of church school term, we had a Sunday school picnic at nearby Marcellus Park, a county-owned park at the time. Our family attended and shared a pot luck lunch; dessert was a variety of homemade cookies and cakes with inch-high frosting. The park had a concrete swimming pool and attached kiddie pool with a small sprinkler in the center. After the picnic and games, we headed to the pool at the north end of the park. Older kids swam in the three-foot end and babies and toddlers waded in the shallow end of the forty-foot pool. Because of safety concerns, upkeep, budgets, and expensive insurance, the pool closed in the mid-1960's.

An exciting time for the whole family was the church Christmas pageant held on the Sunday evening closest to Christmas.

Social Calendar

A play was presented on the biblical story of the birth of Christ. Angels, wise men, Mary, Joseph and Jesus were roles for children from age-appropriate Sunday school classes. Costumes were made by talented seamstresses in the congregation. "Silent Night" was the closing hymn, with lighted candles throughout the sanctuary, a custom still observed at our Christmas Eve service. After the pageant, we went to the church basement to await the anticipated arrival of Santa Claus. When he entered through the back entrance he rang a handheld bell and carried a red velvet bag filled with wrapped books. Santa shook each of our hands and wished us a "Merry Christmas, Ho, Ho, Ho!" as he passed through the excited crowd of children. Each left with a red mesh stocking filled with candy and a new book, after enjoying homemade Christmas cookies and hot chocolate. We were happy!

Even though my parents were Grange members, they did not attend meetings regularly. Grange had been around for nearly a century as a social outlet for farmers with programs and education sponsored by the government. While growing up we had a local Grange in Onondaga Hill and South Onondaga, with covered dish picnics in the summer and harvest dinners in the fall. Also, a fall sale was held when farmers brought extra produce to be auctioned off for a fundraiser. Mom and Dad went and bought apples, squash or homemade baked goods. Throughout the years, as the small farmer disappeared from the landscape, Grange membership ebbed and the two Grange facilities near our home were sold to other organizations.

Our small South Onondaga Fire Department was dependent on local farmers to serve the community when emergency calls came in, but services such as ambulances and medical emergency help still had to come from the city, and the wait time could be half an hour or more. The volunteer farmers were trained to handle fires and available during the day throughout the district; neighbors depended on them for quick responses. Farmers felt good about reaching out to help others in need, and the community was comfortable knowing a fire truck would show up during daytime hours when many non-farmers were away at jobs in the city. Dad had a grass fire one time near his barns, and with the firefighters' quick response the fire was put out without spreading to them.

Trained EMTs were not available during the 1950's and 60's. When I was in third grade, a boy one grade ahead of me was swinging at a bee and fell out of a second-story window in our school. Minutes later, watching from buses lined up along Route 80 to take us home; we could see him on the ground covered with a sheet, the nurse and other school personnel waiting for emergency help from the city to arrive. Fortunately, he survived with broken bones. Today EMTs arrive within minutes.

Small fire houses (with one engine and one tanker) that served local communities have now disappeared. Today large updated fire departments housing multiple fire engines, emergency trucks and other facilities are more capable of handling emergencies.

Social Calendar

They also are used for community events, help support local schools, and provide a place for clubs, weddings, and fundraisers.

Each year our family looked forward to attending the local firemen's field days throughout the area. We didn't have much money, but carefully selected a few special treats – some rides and cotton candy or a candy apple. Amusement rides, beer and bingo tents, carnival games, sausage sandwiches, salt potatoes, and grand parades brought communities together for summer fun. Fire departments scheduled their annual field days to not conflict with other nearby departments' annual events. As years went by, the field days dwindled to the point of disappearing in most communities, due to lack of manpower, cost of insurance, and new interests in the community.

A neighbor, Alberta Alexander, wrote news items for the local *Marcellus Observer* about local happenings, illnesses or accidents concerning country folks in our community. Included in the column were anniversaries, birthdays, special trips, and other news of interest about neighbors, letting people know what was going on, especially if someone was sick and needed a casserole or homemade dessert.

Other than attending one or two Sunday clambakes during the summer, Mom and Dad stayed home seven nights a week, except for an occasional car ride on country roads observing progress other farmers were making growing crops, or checking out a new barn being built. Dad took Mom out to dinner for their anniversary, a rare treat – eating in restaurants was far too expensive and not common for anyone.

We went to Aunt Betty Luchsinger's on Bussey Road for our haircuts. Her steady hand did an excellent job trimming our hair and cutting straight bangs across foreheads. This was also a social gathering, as Dad and Uncle Fred visited and we played in the yard with cousins.

Mom and Dad were proud that my sisters Beverly and Heidi tried out for the Onondaga County Dairy Princess pageant that was held every June. The winner had to commit to travel and had speaking engagements throughout the county, and also spent time at the New York State Fair promoting dairy products. In 1970, Beverly was crowned princess and promoted dairy products in the inner-city Head Start program. Each day she took along a small dairy barn and silo, and little bags of hay, corn, silage, and wheat for the children to see and touch. The little girls all wanted to be princesses. She also served milk punch and cheese at P&C grocery stores. Heidi, crowned in 1979, did similar projects with small children, visiting schools. She was a guest on television, rode on floats in parades, and had speaking engagements at dairy meetings.

After Mom started working, she squirreled away a little of her earnings for a well-deserved vacation. One time she received information on farm tours with the specific interests of farmers in mind. Mom gently persuaded Dad to sign up for one of these tours out of Auburn. She planned for coverage for all the family and farm

Social Calendar

chores, did the packing, and had some money saved. These trips turned out to be the experiences of a lifetime. After the initial tour they became a yearly event, giving my parents the opportunity to visit California, Florida, Canada, Hawaii, the Grand Canyon, the Mid-West, and beyond. They visited pineapple fields, wineries, and many other dairy farms. Tours were farm-themed and included lodging, meals, transportation, and sightseeing stops each day. They ate well, Dad rested, and they made friends. Mom used to say, "When farmers get together they are never lost for words!" When they arrived home, they talked about their trip for months.

A sense of community has been lost with the absence the small farmer. Old traditions are sometimes lost, and not replaced with new ones. Some of our dearest traditions centered on Christmas. Today it seems to be all about buying, but a short time ago it was far more meaningful...

Social Calendar

Chapter 28

Christmas!

As young children, dreaming of a white Christmas was the furthest thing from our minds – never mind the snow, it was all about presents! After school shopping in the fall, the only time we received new clothes was at Christmas. Mom would say, "Wait for Christmas! If you are good, maybe Santa Claus will bring it!"

Mom and Dad tried hard to give us whatever we really wanted – toys, clothes, candy. And they did! Our Christmases were awesome. Mom made sure everyone received equally and each received that special "wish list" item. If the request was impossible, she warned us that the item we asked for was not practical. But sometimes she told us that and then surprised us with the gift under the tree!

Catalogs arrived in early November. My sisters, brothers and I would leaf through the pages for hours huddled around the central furnace, talking with Mom about Christmas wishes. (Mom made mental notes with sharp ears and good listening skills.) As we older children stopped believing in Santa, we teased younger siblings about seeing him in the window or reminded them "to be good or

Christmas!

Santa won't stop at our house!"

One time I found a list in Mom's purse of items for each child and check-offs. This is how she did it! She made lists! But how did she shop for so much? Little did I know, Mom did a lot of mail ordering through Montgomery Ward and Sears, and then hid the merchandise at Grandma Tilden's house.

As a very young child I remember nothing being wrapped; we came down the stairs and there the items were, nicely arranged under the tree. At some point we requested the presents be wrapped so Christmas would last longer, and another job was added to Mom's list of things to do!

Our Christmas tree was always fresh cut, from Dad's brother John who sold at the Regional Market for decades. Dad made sure there was no artificial tree in our house! Mom assigned me to decorate the tree, and I carefully placed one tinsel icicle at a time over each branch of the tree. Younger siblings wanted to help and I patiently let them; when they weren't looking I redid their work.

Other than the Christmas pageant at church or a concert at school, few outside functions were on our family agenda. We envied other families who made fancy Christmas cookies but simple sugar cookies with pink or green frosting were a welcome treat. We enjoyed what we had as special ingredients were hard to add to our grocery budget.

The Christmas pageant was held at church one or two weeks before Christmas. But Karen, Bev, and I would plan, practice, and Christmas!

present our own Christmas program for our parents. Sometimes we would have this event in the archway between the living and dining rooms. For weeks we rehearsed songs that we found in the World Book Encyclopedia, memorizing "Silent Night," "It Came Upon the Midnight Clear," "Joy To The World," and others. We selected one of the younger kids to be in the manager and other sisters to be angels. (There was a lot of fun and resourcefulness, but we were still picked on or mocked by our brothers!) We dragged Dad upstairs where another stage was made with sheets and blankets. We had limited supplies, but improvising was a valuable lesson learned while growing up.

    Every Christmas Eve Mom would make Dad oyster stew served with oyster crackers, a tradition he had as a child growing up. Scalloped oysters were sometimes served. I never cared for either, but liked the flavorful buttery broth. After supper we went to Dad's dresser and picked out his stretched-out gray hunting socks with a red ring around the top for us to hang at the end of the couch with our names on paper pinned on the outside.

    Christmas Eve night was long, very long! Hours dragged by before we finally went to sleep. Secretly Dad drove to Grandma's house to retrieve the presents and Mom and Dad quickly, and quietly, placed them under the tree. Dad was dragging by then – his bedtime was always around nine o'clock. He liked routines and stayed within a specified time frame for everything he did – going to bed, eating meals, planting his crops. He learned this from his Christmas!

father. A late night venture was not in his schedule; he still had to get up at 5:30 a.m. to milk cows and do chores.

As we were all snuggled in our beds, sugar plums DID dance in our heads! My sister Karen would rustle awake about 3 a.m., and decide it would be "great" if everyone shared in the anticipation. Soon all of us were moving from room to room telling younger sisters to get up. We had a large square hall outside the five bedrooms, and as each one awoke we gathered there where card games, board games, or quiet talk began. (When we got too loud, Dad would yell up and tell us plain and simple, "shut up!") About 4:30 a.m. the youngest was sent downstairs to our parent's bedroom to beg Mom to let us come down, and then she quickly returned, with a "Mom said no!" Not giving up, a few minutes later another younger one reluctantly went downstairs; again she returned saying, "Mom said 5:30." By 5:15 the whole household was awake and the ok was given. The long-anticipated morning had finally arrived. Hurrying downstairs, we stopped and gasped at all the presents under the tree and for the next half-hour there was mayhem, with loud voices, laughter, and screeching with delight. Younger siblings were dazed, and older ones savored the moment. Most gifts were wrapped, but several dolls were often visible under the tree. One Christmas three of us received bride dolls. Another year I received a wished-for portable typewriter and my sister Karen received a record player. My brothers might receive a basketball, a BB gun, or a 22 caliber rifle, depending on age. Santa delivered many much-needed Christmas!

wishes including new outfits for school. After the thrill of opening presents we looked in our stockings, each bulging with mittens, a tangerine, trinkets or a necklace, and a good-sized candy cane.

Quickly after the gifts were unwrapped and stockings emptied, Dad announced, "Time for chores!" and my brothers headed to the barn, already half an hour behind schedule. My sisters and I spent the morning playing with the toys and games, and at some point I was ushered into the kitchen to help with the big Christmas dinner planned for about one o'clock. Always on the menu were turkey, dressing, mashed potatoes, vegetables, jello salad, rolls and pie, all homemade. Grandma Tilden came for dinner and she brought each of us a wrapped package containing a comb and one dollar with a tiny candy cane taped to the outside. We thought we had a million dollars! We also received a pair of socks from Great-Grandma Wadsworth until her death in 1961.

At 4:30 p.m. the evening milking and chores began. (Dairy farmers never got a day off, even Christmas!) Supper was leftover turkey and trimmings. Bedtime was a little earlier than usual – we were exhausted from lack of sleep from the night before. Year after year we enjoyed the same pleasant routine of dreaming, making wish lists, and teasing our siblings. Christmas memories still touch our souls with joy and happiness.

Christmas came "but once a year." The rest of the year was mainly hard work.

Christmas!

Chapter 29

Dad's Endless Jobs

Feeding our family, purchasing clothing, and providing a warm comfortable home weighed heavily on our parents. Food stamps, free or reduced lunches at school, and free health care were not available during our era (we would have qualified). Thankfully, Dad and Mom were taught by their parents how to improvise and be resourceful.

With never-ending vet bills, a volatile milk market, expensive repair bills, and replacement costs for farm equipment, costly feed for animals, gas for tractors, medical bills, car, mortgage, and insurance payments, it was a huge financial challenge to raise eight kids. Mom and Dad rented the Tilden farm from 1943, after the death of Great-Grandpa Tilden, until 1959. When Grandpa Luchsinger died in 1959, each of his children inherited three thousand dollars, and Dad used his money as a down payment on the farm. After all those years of renting, Mom and Dad finally owned their own place! They continued to pay Grandma Tilden the monthly mortgage payment on the farm, a financial blessing as she lived on a small social security check. When she died in 1971 at the age of 64 after a long battle with cancer, they still owed a little on the farm. Mom's four brothers relinquished the remainder of the mortgage because Mom had cared for Grandma around the clock for many months instead of placing her in a nursing home.

Besides managing the dairy farm, Dad was employed away from home to make ends meet. He believed if you looked for work and were not fussy you could find it. A job provided money, but sitting on your behind because you didn't particularly like an aspect of the job wouldn't put cash in your pocket. He used to repeat the common expression, "A dollar earned is a dollar saved."

Resourcefulness and spirit shaped how our parents found ways to provide for our family. Early in Mom and Dad's marriage they picked up potatoes after they were dug with a potato digger, at the Rohe Farm on Rohe Road at three cents a bushel. Sometimes they would make $4.50 for the day. "Good money!" he said. "Cash in your pocket is a good thing!" Dad had the stamina and dedication to labor long hours every day without complaining. When he found employment away from the farm – either short or long-term, he had to be flexible and available when a call came.

In the early 1950's Dad worked for Ward's Feed Store on Erie Boulevard unloading feed off railroad cars. One-hundred-pound feed bags were loaded onto dolly carts on a tract and moved to the storage area. Often he was called into work with short notice when railroad cars came into town and extra help was needed. He also worked at Auburn Beacon in the feed mill during their busy

Dad's Endless Jobs

season, with the backbreaking job of unloading and stacking heavy bags of feed. But Dad never grumbled about work; he felt mentally and physically well about working. For many years he milked cows, fed livestock, cleaned the barn, and then headed to the city for his 8:00 to 4:30 construction job. Then (unlike his colleagues) he headed back home, milked his herd of Jerseys, and did the evening chores. Finally he came to the dinner table at 6:30, repeating this ritual five days a week. Dad criticized lazy people, especially recruits showing up for work but finding excuses to stand around. He also observed workers who looked for easy jobs requiring little manual labor, avoiding sweat or dirt, or afraid to deal with the weather – heat, cold, snow, or rain.

Winter Around the Farm

Dad worked for the Town of Onondaga as a substitute driver or wingman on the snowplows, especially during long periods of extended snowstorms. We were excited when Dad received a call to go to work; a little extra pay meant a little something extra we needed or paid a bill. Sometimes he waved or blew the horn when driving by in the enormous snowplow.

With what appeared to be Swiss inborn talent, Dad could build anything! He worked at Syracuse University through a connection with neighbor Dave Anderson, a professor in the Forestry Department. Dad said their model was to tear down and build up even if change was unnecessary. He felt a person should not fix or repair anything that doesn't need fixing. Even though it was a waste of money in his eyes, however, Dad didn't complain because he was grateful to make good money.

Dad had a job with the early construction of Community General Hospital at Upstate making footers (wooden frames made to hold concrete). He was present when the first load of concrete was poured, sharing the excitement with fellow workers.

During the 1960's, Dad helped construct the Money Building and Emerson Museum in Syracuse, working many stories up. He never feared height and walked around the edge without a safety harness. I'm not sure if Dad refused to wear a harness or regulations didn't require it. He said everyone down below looked like little ants.

Dad also worked for his brother Pete building houses and barns throughout Onondaga and Marcellus. On car rides he often pointed out that he helped build a barn or house. He enjoyed remodeling kitchens for friends and family, and even built two entire homes, Mort's and mine! Dad was self-taught but he could read blueprints, measure, cut, pound, and lug effortlessly. Besides milking cows, planting, and harvesting he hurried through breakfast and headed out to other jobs to support our family.

Dad took calves to the auction in Sennet to make a dollar or two. Once he took two Jersey calves hoping to net twenty dollars. At the time beef prices were rock bottom and after the commission and beef promotion fees he ended up paying $4.29.

Sometimes Dad bartered services for goods. It wasn't unusual for Dad to cut and bale hay for the semi-retired neighbors in exchange for some of the hay or credit towards rent. Other times he would plow a small area of a field and in return be able to use additional acres for himself.

Dad was amazing. He taught us that work never harmed anyone, and he was able to work fifteen – hour days because he ate healthy, slept well, never smoked or drank and had no bad habits that could harm him. Mom sometimes got annoyed with him because he could "shut off his motor" at bedtime, while she tossed and turned, worrying about family business.

Grandpa and Grandma Luchsinger had also worked as a team, always looking for innovative ways to pay bills, so Dad witnessed survival techniques first hand. Grandpa Luchsinger had to learn the English language, work long hours, and be thrifty with his earnings and spending. He had ideas and vision, and my father did too!

Dad's Endless Jobs

Chapter 30

The Blizzard of '66

January 28, 1966, driving home to Syracuse in my standard shift 1965 Dodge Dart, relief whirled in my head, as I had just finished my last exam for the semester at SUNY Morrisville. One more semester until graduation! Exhilaration filled me as I left campus with my usual bag of dirty laundry. I have a full week without worry, studying, writing papers, tests, and the dreaded walk across campus, wearing the required skirt with cold wind beating against my bare legs.

The car radio playing Elvis and the Beatles soothed my thoughts; the newscaster warned of a blizzard heading our way. No worries – I was used to ice, slippery roads, and five-foot snow banks. My only fear living in Central New York was blinding snow. Nineteen-year-olds don't think much about the what ifs.

When I arrived home mid-afternoon from my forty-mile drive from college, my six younger siblings greeted me at the door. Relief was written all over my mother's face. Storm warnings were being continuously announced on our small black and white television.

Dark skies and bitter cold were the norm for late January, but this storm was not normal. On Saturday, the weather was bitter cold with no evidence of snow. But heavy snow, minus-twenty-six degrees below zero, and sixty mph winds struck us overnight – non-stop arctic winds and blowing snow. Brutal! For three days snow and wind continued to whip about, paralyzing everyone for miles. County snowplows were taken off the highways as they couldn't keep up with high winds and mountains of white stuff developing into drifts and snowbanks stretching up to the telephone wires. The oil furnace in our one-hundred-fifty-year-old two-story, six-bedroom farmhouse struggled to keep our family warm. The outside elements found their way through cracks and single pane windows.

Dad and younger brother Mort tunneled a path to the barn across the road where our herd of Jersey cows had to be milked twice a day. Dad was noticeably worried. Milk was stored in eighty-pound galvanized cans (with a big red three painted on the outside) until the milk truck arrived, but Dad had only enough empty cans for one extra day – then what?

The storm didn't stop us from feeding our family: we had milk, eggs, meat in the freezer, canned vegetables and fruits from our garden, and plenty of homemade jam and peanut butter, plus a supply of day-old bread in the freezer. Typically we went to the grocery store once a week for staples and had plenty to make do.

As the snow showers slowed down, sixty-mile an hour winds continued to play havoc, creating ten-foot drifts. Everyone except

Dad and my brother stayed inside. Two days into the storm there was some bad news. Dad had to dump his cans filled with rich Jersey milk to make room for the next day's milk supply when the truck couldn't get through. No milk shipped, no pay! Money literally down the drain! We struggled financially as it was; this was a big set-back.

Roads were impossible to pass and snowplows were not on the roads. No one knew when they would be opened. Schools closed for the week. My brother Hank was stranded at his apartment in Onondaga Hill with his wife Eileen, of seven months.

My week away from school turned into a week trapped inside with five younger sisters. Mountains of snow had developed into drifts and the biting cold wind was too strong and dangerous for playing outside. Snow reached up over the doors and windows. Sadly, without a choice, Dad continued to dump milk.

By Thursday morning we heard the grunting of the snowplow slowly making a single pass down our country road pushing five to six feet of snow off roads and creating ten to twelve foot banks. Later that day the milk truck driver finally arrived using the narrow path the snowplow created and picked up the fresh milk.

After the driver left, Dad mentioned that he was venturing to Taylor's convenient store just two and a half miles from home. I needed to go, I was not prepared for the storm, and I was out of cigarettes! Against my parents' approval during college I took up smoking; more college students smoked than not, and we didn't really understand the dangers. Smoking was allowed in bars (along with drinking at eighteen) and restaurants, public buildings, academic buildings, hospitals and dorm rooms – almost everywhere.

When Dad and I arrived at the store, to our surprise the shelves were nearly empty. Only Lucky Strikes non-filtered cigarettes were available. It didn't matter – I needed a cigarette even if an occasional piece of tobacco landed in my mouth causing me to spit!

I had no idea my week away from college would be so uneventful (or should I say eventful?) cooped up in a house surrounded by little kids. We had three channels on our black and white TV with rabbit ears (no remote), no Xbox, computer, iPhone, texting, or internet!

Chapter 31

Keeping the Farm

Just two roads away from Dad's farm, $200,000 homes rest on the hillside facing Syracuse city lights, and a view of Syracuse University's dome. Suburbanites readily enjoy fresh country air and the beauty of rural landscapes, trees, and animals roaming through large manicured lawns. The same land my Dad rented and grew corn on only a few years ago sold for thousands of dollars for a three or four-acre lot. Ironically, the farmer who owned this land didn't receive the money; a smart real estate developer waving a handsome sum of money in the face of a tired, debt-ridden farmer bought the whole farm for a few thousand dollars.

Farming had become big business, more mechanized with advanced technology, and often predatory, taking advantage of others by seizing land when neighbor farmers died or weary ones sold their farm for a little cash. Large landowners quickly bought neighboring farms, often adding seventy or eighty acres to their own farm each time a small neighboring farm was on the selling block. If a small farmer wanted to expand, he had no place to go since most of the good farmland was gone. As a result, small family farms which once sprinkled our landscapes have all but disappeared.

Many of my Dad's neighbors were small farmers who were forced to sell. They had tax inequities, taxes that continued to rise, farmland values went down, and market prices fell below farm costs, resulting foreclosures and bankruptcies devastating farming communities. Farming joined big business. Milk prices fluctuated, leaving little or no profit, crops were destroyed by wind and drought, repair bills were in the thousands, and farm children left the farms for easier jobs with secure paychecks.

Family togetherness and commitment was enforced by Dad and we witnessed firsthand the long hours of hard work and financial struggles he endured. Several times as children, we overheard talk of selling the farm; siblings hid within earshot and hung onto every word as Mom and Dad discussed financial options to a bank officer at the dining room table in the next room. Thoughts of moving and leaving the security and warmth of our home and neighbors hit us like a ton of bricks. Afraid that we might move to a different school and lose sharing chores and daily routines was overwhelming.

But Dad believed life on the farm was perfect for raising a family and selling out and moving was not an option in his mind. He understood the pain he'd suffer if he had to leave what he loved and worked for. Dad relished being out in the fields and was gratified when he finished a full day of tough work. His cows were his extended family. He persevered even when faced with taxes that continued to go up, milk prices that hit rock bottom, and new government controls that saddled him with financial hardships. Dad just worked harder to pay bills by acquiring jobs away from the farm to fill the gap. He used his inherent carpentry skills and also sold Christmas trees and pumpkins for extra income.

Pumpkins for Sale

Dad stayed optimistic, hoping the price of milk would go up and the weather cooperate. He found good help from local teenage boys who were willing to work and he relied on his children, even though we didn't enjoy the tedious labor of farm work. As teenagers, my sisters and I worked at Pfeiffer's Drive-In Restaurant as soon as we could. We received minimum wage, made friends, had regular days and nights off, and had a job physically less grueling. But most important, we had paychecks to spend on clothing, or cars, or put away for college. This took some of the burden off Dad and Mom.

When Dad was growing up each of his six siblings worked from morning until nightfall, and then they married and had their own farms. But our generation was different – we were looking for ways to leave the farm. Our friends came from suburban, middle class families who had jobs in Syracuse at Chrysler, General Electric, General Motors, or the New York Central Railroad. Some parents of our friends were professionals such as nurses, teachers, engineers, or lawyers. We looked forward to leaving the farm for secure paychecks and good jobs.

Dad did everything possible to make ends meet. He tried improving techniques in farming and but stayed away from unnecessary purchasing of new equipment or livestock. But Dad was reluctant to take financial risks to expand his farm or keep up with expensive technology. He tried to survive on his own terms. Mom helped by working at Beak and Skiff Orchards (many women did go to work to help with bills and receive medical coverage) and Dad supplemented his income working on construction during the week. We continued to grow our own vegetables and raised our own beef to feed our family of ten and the workload was never-ending.

As we grew up, Dad continued to farm. Cows not producing young or too old to generate a sufficient amount of milk were sold to local butchers. When our family needed meat, a cow was sent to the slaughterhouse. First came home the fresh liver wrapped in brown butcher paper, sometimes still warm, then the tongue and heart.

Nights that we had these delicacies, I went to bed hungry. (We ate what was on the table or went without.) The remainder of the cow was picked up at the slaughterhouse and delivered to a meat cutter who cut up the meat for our family freezer.

Dad couldn't compete with the "new" farmer. There were too many high cost risks and better job opportunities offered away from the struggling farm, and the pressure from urban society affected us siblings. The market, malls, advertising, and benefits of working elsewhere have enticed us to seek gainful employment away from the farm. I did what I could and learned how to earn money away from home.

1940 Combine used on the Farm until 2016

Chapter 32

Mary Goes To Work

Children in farm families worked from the time we understood directions and were mature enough to handle responsibilities. Parents taught us at a young age how to properly clean, cook, babysit, can and freeze, wallpaper, garden, milk cows, load hay, or drive a tractor. We were expected to help without complaint, allowances, or rewards.

At eleven, babysitting for neighbors and relatives was my first real job. Being the eldest of six girls, I was a valued commodity! I knew right from wrong and I was cheap – thirty-five cents an hour, sometimes fifty. I never set the salary, but accepted whatever pay was given, as working itself was important experience. Most of my babysitting money was squandered on clothes and other things young girls desired. Once I bought a plaid wool skirt for seven dollars (a lot of money) at Lerner's. There was a school rule that the hem on a skirt could not be above the knee; fearful of being questioned about the length, I walked with a crowd or hunched over when passing an authority!

I helped the family by selling Christmas cards door to door.

Neighbors and relatives traditionally sent out cards yearly in the 1950's and 60's, so every summer from the time I was ten or eleven I walked up and down country roads taking orders for Christmas cards at fifty cents a box. I carried samples along with Christmas wrapping paper and had customers write their names on the bottom of the boxes. Usually women would buy two or three boxes. Mom got to keep the free sample boxes for her own use, and the money I made was used, along with babysitting money, to buy school clothes. One year I even earned enough to buy much-needed eyeglasses.

    Jobs were scarce for teenagers in 1962 – there were a few fast food places and only a couple of strip malls around Syracuse. Fortunately, at sixteen I was hired at Pfeiffer's Drive-In as a waitress and eventually was trained for other jobs, including cooking and preparing to open on Sunday. Being a three-season restaurant, Pfeiffer's was a perfect job for a teenager, and working there my last two years of high school and summers while attending college helped with expenses and clothing. I saved every penny I could for college. The salary was a whopping $1.15 an hour; tips only seventy-five cents or one dollar each night. (With counter service, most people did not tip.) I worked a full forty hours, a nice steady income. Dad always said, "There's work if you look for it!" and I found it.

    In early winter, my first semester at Morrisville, I answered an ad posted in the dorm office to work in a private home for several months while the mother had eye surgery and recuperated at home.

Mary Goes To Work

The job paid $1.25 an hour. After classes I walked over a mile through the town, past the cemetery to a ranch home, my bare legs exposed to the bitter cold. (Wearing a skirt was required to attend classes, and I walked directly from class to my job. Going back to the dorm to change into something warmer took too long.)

Each day when I arrived, the house was always unlocked – no fear of break-ins or murderers lurking in the cellar in the tiny village of Morrisville! Besides that, the NY State Trooper barracks were just up the street. A list of suggested duties laid on the table, which often included ironing 3XL white dress shirts for the man of the house, a teacher at the local high school. I also cleaned the house thoroughly. Sometimes I made homemade spaghetti sauce, thawing out meat from their freezer. Their daughter, six-year-old Susan, once asked me to make her a birthday cake, which I did. Being a little homesick for my own family, I occasionally accepted an invitation to stay for dinner and welcomed Mr. Jenks' offer to drive me back to the dorm. My training at home had given me the skills to admirably take over a household, doing the cooking, cleaning, and ironing with confidence. Another lesson from my parents was, "The best way you learn is by doing."

During my second year at college I worked fifteen hours a week in a work-study program. I typed for a professor and sat at a desk in the dorm office answering the phone and monitoring the sign-in/sign-out sheets while doing my homework. I was paid $1.25 an hour, giving me $60 plus a month. I saved for incidentals and put the rest in the bank.

Because I had some money in my bank account and had learned to be frugal from my parents, the idea of purchasing a car was discussed with them. I promised to make monthly payments by working at school, babysitting, and my seasonal job at Pfeiffer's. (I could drive home on weekends to work if I had a car.) Dad took me to a Dodge dealership and after several hours of bickering over the cost we made a deal for a brand new Dodge Dart for $1,925. With a $300 down payment, my monthly car payment was $58. Dad knew how to negotiate, using a few choice words with the salesman; I sheepishly stood in the background, mortified, never quite understanding why Dad and the salesman had to get so nasty. After hours of this tomfoolery I was happy when an agreement was finally made, and while heading home Dad chuckled, talking about the sale and telling me how to buy a car.

Within days of graduating from SUNY Morrisville at the old age of nineteen, the task of finding a real job began. There was no sitting around for the summer or going to Europe to "find myself." I knew who I was! General Electric, the largest employer in Syracuse at the time, was hiring in 1966. I drove the forty-five minutes from home to the General Electric employment office and entered a large room filled with prospective new hires, fearful and nervous. These were grown up people; this was the real deal! I was asked to fill out an application, sitting in the room with rows and rows of chairs filled to capacity, with fifty to sixty other women of all ages. Men were in another room.

I dressed in proper attire wearing a blue suit, heels, stockings, and some jewelry including clip earrings, all appropriate for a job interview. After sitting down, I looked around, noticing others wearing simple slacks and plain tops, and some were smoking. Later I realized these potential employees were looking for factory work. Finally, a neat, cheerful woman (in a perfect suit, stockings, and heels) called my name and introduced herself to me as Bonnie. We had an informal visit and I was then directed to another area for more interviews and typing and shorthand tests, then directed back to Bonnie's office. She was confident I would be called within a few days for another interview for a specific secretarial job. (In the 1960's we were called secretaries; now the job title is administrative assistants.)

Within days I was called for an interview at the Semiconductor Department, Building 7. When I met the manager, I kept telling myself to relax, proceed with confidence, and smile. A two-year degree in Secretarial Science, working hard in a farm family, and a lot of maturity helped me through. I met several engineers and told them I enjoyed working with numbers. Wow! The best thing I could have said! They asked me to add up a list of numbers in my head; fortunately, even under pressure I answered correctly. (I often had to add numbers on paper and in my head as a waitress.) Within a few days they offered me the job! My starting salary as a grade-five secretary was approximately one hundred dollars a week. (At that time gas was twenty-nine cents a gallon and new cars cost two thousand dollars.) I lived at home and paid five dollars weekly rent and helped with chores and cooking.

I worked at General Electric for seven years, enjoying my job working with one manager and twenty engineers. My job consisted lots of typing, phone answering, scheduling, and some shorthand. I was promoted several times to secretarial positions in manufacturing, personnel, and transportation departments.

In 1968, I married Clifford Sperling and started saving for a house, depositing every one of my paychecks each week toward a down payment on a future home. With my dad's carpentry skills and my husband's talents in plumbing and electrical we built our home on a half-acre lot, part of the family farm. I had become accustomed to budgets and sacrificing, and envisioned being a stay-at-home mom. After three and a half years of marriage, our first son Dan was born and I fulfilled that dream.

But...within a few months of Dan's birth, Dad approached me with an opportunity to clean the church every Friday. They were desperate to have someone clean seven hours a week at two dollars an hour. Dad's job as Building and Grounds chairperson at the church was to find someone. I could take Dan along with me, so I did and cleaned until Steve was born two years later.

Before Steve was born, I took a cake-decorating course at BOCES and got lots of practice making cakes for my extended family. The word got out that the cakes were professional-looking

Mary Goes To Work

and delicious. Making them for the public led me to making pies, hors d'oeuvres, and wedding cakes, and with my love for cooking, I started a catering business two years later. My sisters Bev and Chris helped, and occasionally Heidi and Karen working as a team, getting the food prepared and served. I kept busy lugging heavy pans of food and preparing exclusively homemade food for Masonic Men's monthly dinners, weddings, luncheons at senior citizen centers and churches all over the county. Meanwhile I had two more sons, Matt and Tim! I needed to stay focused and organized since my husband worked the afternoon shift for many years; babysitters helped until they were old enough to be home alone.

One of my many, many cakes

In 1986, I was diagnosed with cancer and needed surgery and a few months' recovery. Our sons, now, 3, 7, 11, and 13 and my husband Cliff gave me lots of love and support. I healed, determined to get right back into the mix of things, but my husband told me I was working too hard, and catering was basically killing me. But, I thought, how can anyone work too hard? Work was part of who I was – my legacy from Grandpa and Dad. I loved to work!

To solve this dilemma, I told Cliff I was going back to school full-time to become a home economics teacher. (Mom had wanted to be a teacher but was unable to fulfill her dream.) Endless days as children, my sisters and I had played school, with me playing the role as teacher. Why not? Perfect timing – Tim was soon starting kindergarten. I was 42; after completing the required courses I would be 45 – if I went back or not! After some research, however, I found that the only school near my home with a major in home economics was one hundred miles away. So, I focused on plan B – English and Elementary, and attended the local community college only four miles from home to complete nineteen credits before transferring to Cortland State, driving thirty-five miles each way to complete my bachelors. I was determined, and worked hard taking care of four kids, sometimes going to bed when they did and getting up at 4 a.m. to study, finish homework or write papers, working hard to get A's and become a teacher.

Mary Goes To Work

1990 – Mom throws a party for the graduate

After completing my bachelor's degree and graduating cum laude, the state required me to get my master's degree within three years. Doing substitute teaching and working on my Master's in Reading, I persevered and in 1993, was offered the K-12 Reading Specialist position at Onondaga Central School. Besides teaching Reading, some years I taught Family and Consumer Science (Home Economics) one period a day, along with Writing and English until retirement in 2008. My only regret is that I didn't do it sooner.

It was important that our four sons were taught life skills, to be dependable and have a good work ethic. They jumped at the opportunity to work on the farm when they were old enough to earn a little cash. The work was tough! My father was tough! (They didn't have to lift weights for football; they had lots of training stacking bales of hay.) Our sons respected the farm work and their grandfather. A few years ago, our oldest son Dan, gave his grandfather a handsome sum of money for Christmas. Grandpa thought he was rich. Dan said, "No, Grandpa, you taught me how to work, and I am forever thankful!"

When my boys wanted steadier paychecks in high school and during college, they worked at Wegmans, Blockbuster, Valvoline, or bartended at Links at Sunset Ridge, adding more skills to become productive adults. When they attended college, we reinforced basic rules – finish in four years and learn a saleable skill. Today each son has his own success story – all work hard like their parents, grandparents and great-grandparents. Dan is a Supervisor in Nuclear Medicine, Steve is in Aerospace, Matt is an Industrial Mechanic, and Tim is in Computed Tomography.

1990 – Cortland Colledge Graduation with my huband and four sonds

Chapter 33

Weddings

Mom and Dad joyfully paid for six beautiful weddings for their daughters. Preparations were stress-free: Mom mentored us, straightforward decisions were made, and we were grateful for her guidance. We were not given a budget; we knew and understood our financial limits.

First on our agenda was to establish availability of the church and then set up several meetings with the pastor. Weddings were church-orientated, including a soloist, candles, flowers, and lovely organ music. After setting the date, the next step was to find a reception hall or restaurant (at a reasonable cost) near home that could accommodate the two hundred guests in our huge extended family.

We spent one afternoon shopping for a bridal gown (mine was from Edwards Department Store in downtown Syracuse) and a separate trip to help choose bridesmaid dresses. Local well-established businesses were contacted first with our wedding plans. Meeting with the local florist selecting flowers that went with the color scheme, a five-or-six-tiered vanilla-flavored wedding cake from the Valley Bakery covered with white frosted roses, and simple music, would round-out the planning. Mom coordinated with the groom's mother on the color and length of dresses before our shopping trip. Being budget-minded she never shopped at bridal boutiques, but found the finest dress for the dollar at Sears, Penny's or Edwards. Dad, along with the groomsmen had it easier with matching rented apparel. Proper wedding attire for men was suits, shined up shoes and ties. Women wore dresses with heels and stockings.

Bridal showers were held at someone's home or a church hall and included a simple luncheon or dessert. Gifts were a surprise – there were no bridal registries or wish lists! Sometimes we received duplicates, but were appreciative and returned one for credit. Gifts were thoughtful and practical.

Rehearsal dinners were no big deal – depending on the groom's finances and everyone's busy life. We had pizza at a local diner.

Wedding ceremonies were usually held late Saturday mornings with receptions immediately after. Not only did we have cows to milk, but most of Dad's family were also farmers and had to be home by late afternoon. Two of my sisters, Heidi and Karen, had evening weddings after milking. Wedding pictures were done by a local photographer. A wedding picture was taken of the bride weeks ahead and placed in Sunday's newspaper free of charge the day following the wedding and included a write-up including the parents, dress, education, and employment for both bride and groom.

July 13, 1968 – My Wedding with My Siblings
Back Row from Left: Karen, Hank Jr., Mary (Me), Don, Beverly
Front Row: Shirley, Heidi, Christine

On the day of the wedding, after getting so many family members ready with one bathroom, there was a sign of relief when we all arrived at the church ahead of schedule. Dad proudly walked each of his six daughters down the aisle extending the bride's hand out to each of his new sons-in-law. Emotional as he was, Dad would manage a smile through his tears. Our long, white wedding gowns filled the aisle along with bouquets of seasonal flowers. Floral arrangements at the altar were quickly moved after the ceremony to the wedding reception's head table.

Our reception luncheons were served buffet style and included salads, cold cuts, cheese, rolls, relishes, and maybe one or two hot dishes. Tables were covered with linens. Fruited punch, spiked punch, and beer served; an open bar was not in our budget. We had a toast, danced, and threw the bouquet and garter. Dad paid for the reception, selling some hay or using part of his monthly milk check. When our two brothers married, the bride's family paid for the reception. Traditionally, the groom paid for flowers, church, and pastor.

1982 – Mom and Dad's 40th Anniversary
From Left: Don, Chris, Karen, Shirley, Mom, Dad, Mary (Me), Heidi, Bev, Hank Jr.

Weddings were much simpler during the 1960's –70's. We had no wedding planner, no pedicures, table flowers, or favors (just colorful mints wrapped in netting) save the date cards, limousines,

Weddings

food and dessert tasting sessions, pre-wedding hair styling appointments or weekend bachelor or bachelorette getaways.

1992 – Mom and Dad's 50th Anniversary

We didn't forget Mom and Dad over the years – we had parties for their 25th, 40th, 50th, and 60th wedding anniversaries always hoping for another. In 1973, we lured Mom and Dad to a surprise anniversary party at my home with Uncle Fred and Aunt

Betty Luchsinger, and surprised them all with well-deserved air tickets to Switzerland!

*1973 –We're going to Switzerland!!
From Left: Uncle Fred, Aunt Betty, Dad, Mom*

Weddings

Chapter 34

For The Love of Farming

My dad loved farming. But how could he? No insurance, no sick days, no overtime pay, ninety-hour work weeks, no pension, no medical leave or paid vacations – in fact, no vacation at all, including Christmas and Thanksgiving! But Dad never complained about the bitter cold of winter in upstate New York or sweltering heat in summer, although sometimes he wished for a gentle all-day rain to foster his crops, or prayed for a little longer growing season before frost ended summer.

Before sunrise each day Dad headed to the barn to start morning chores, and feed 150 Jersey livestock before milking. During spring, summer, and fall, everyone took brief breakfast, lunch, and dinner breaks, then went back to the fields to work. On occasion, a flicker of a light in the barn was seen past midnight. A cow might be delivering a calf, or Dad could be checking to see if the water pipes were freezing.

Dad never grumbled about hard manual work or difficult working conditions, even though the elements played havoc with him – the heat of summer with sunburn and the raw cold of winter.

Cash was always short, but in his words, "Farming keeps you alive." He kept moving, never planned on retiring, and often reminded us to "Get off your seat and move your feet! People die if they retire and sit around!" At 92, Dad was still working in the fields, plowing, picking corn, and baling hay, putting in six to eight hours each day. Work was Dad's play and a source of success and self-expression. He had a generous heart, loved his family, his animals, his land, and the freedom of being his own boss, like his father, the Swiss immigrant.

Dad's still bailing hay at 90

Dad had dreams and visions despite unexpected difficulties. While driving the tractor in the fields he thought about the future, looking for resourceful ways to meet never-ending bills. He needed to expand his dairy herd, but first needed a larger barn to house his cows and hay. In 1958, for a little extra cash, Dad had ten acres of his fine hardwoods logged. Using his ingenuity, he bartered with a lumber company and had timber set aside for an eighty-foot addition to the barn he was planning to build the next season. Logs were dragged from the woods by a lumberjack outfit to the nearby road for storing until a larger lumber truck hauled them off, leaving Dad with a portion for his barn-building project. Dad repeatedly loaded three logs at a time onto a wagon and delivered them to a sawmill on Holmes Road a short distance away, coming back with a load of cut lumber from the previous load of logs.

Sharing his ambition with Mom and with a carpenter's pencil in hand, Dad planned and designed the new barn he was going to attach to the old cow barn. Next he marked out the dimensions using posts of rough lumber. My father worked on the barn during any free moment. Using a small hand-turned mixer to blend the sand, cement, fine gravel, and water, he made just enough batches for the three or four hours he had to spare between doing other chores. After pouring the footers and letting them set, he positioned concrete blocks, flawlessly measuring and leveling each block as it was set in place. Dad worked fast but efficiently until he had the foundation, windows, and doorway openings in place. He worked diligently to complete this portion of the barn, determined to get the first floor completed and capped before winter.

2000 – The Barns that Dad built

Dad worked when he could during the winter building stanchions, troughs, and gutters for the new portion of the barn; he also worked other jobs to earn cash. The next spring he started with the hayloft segment, building rafters by hand and, with extra manpower from my brothers and hired teenagers, nailed them in place. The tin roof he put on skillfully, working fearlessly on a ladder thirty or forty feet up.

In 1962, Dad rebuilt the old part of the barn. In 1986, as the needs of the farm grew, Dad added another sixty-foot to the original barn. As was the custom of most small farmers, he used his carpentry talents and relied on his sons and neighbor kids for labor during construction.

For nearly fifty years Dad sold pumpkins at the farm. We had "pick your own" for a while – cars were parked up and down each side of the road and families had a great time exploring the field and picking pumpkins at twenty-five cents. After a couple of years with early snow or heavy frost Dad was discouraged with the "pick your own" pumpkin business. If the weatherman predicted a freeze, Dad had us kids go to the field hustling around cutting stems and placing pumpkins in piles. Then we covered them with a heavy layer of straw to keep the cold from turning them to mush. Dad thought it was easier to pick and grade pumpkins, put them in rows by the corncrib and cover them with canvas at dusk, rather than a last-minute rush to get the pumpkins under cover. We had less waste and fewer broken stems if we picked pumpkins, but it was more labor intense. Dad also sold decorative gourds, squash, corn stalks, straw, and Indian corn.

A labor of love

Eventually Dad moved the pumpkins to a pole barn under cover and we helped as a team to make attractive displays for customers. City folks came out to the farm to enjoy the rural setting and country atmosphere. Sometimes they asked to see the cows and take pictures for their memory-making albums. For the fifty years Dad sold pumpkins my brothers, sisters, and I helped pick and sell and visited with the customers, and many came back. We didn't want or expect wages – just to help and meet friendly people. Years later the same customers often stopped and asked if the nice little old man was still alive. Chuckling, we might say, "Yes, he's in the office taking a nap!"

Dad made a few bucks selling raw milk (unpasteurized). Drinking raw milk sounds undesirable, but we drank it directly from the cooler for decades with no ill effects. Two or three acquaintances from the city came to the farm to purchase raw milk for their families each week; they brought their own jugs, and Dad carefully poured the amount requested into their containers. A couple of dollars from each visit came in handy.

In the sixties and seventies Dad sold Christmas trees at the farm. Dad's brother John bought hundreds of well-groomed trees wholesale to sell at the Regional Market in Syracuse. Dad bought some from Uncle John and sold his trees from the shed next to the corncribs that had earlier stored wagonloads of pumpkins. If weather permitted, a few trees were displayed outside, neatly leaning against hay wagons for customers to view. He wisely sold only a few select trees, but "When they're gone, they're gone!" he said, and he wasn't stuck with leftover trees. Dad's brother Ed also sold trees for years from his farm in Lafayette, and his family continues to do so. As years went by other farmers and local businesses sold Christmas trees and set up pumpkin stands that included hayrides, refreshments, face painting and other amusements – expanding their businesses into fantasy worlds for young children and parents young at heart.

Dad's love for farming never wavered, even though there were days he was discouraged with problems and frustrations. He never threw up his arms and quit; never lost his spirit or motivation. He faced raw weather, often worked without a profit, but continued to be optimistic, enthusiastic, and proud of being a farmer. But the greatest challenges of his life were yet to come.

Chapter 35

Coping With Loss

In early summer of 2003 something was seriously wrong with Mom. Dad noticed a change in demeanor a few months before she shared her concerns. After several visits to doctors and outside testing, Mom was admitted to the hospital. During her stay and after many tests and biopsies, a diagnosis was finally confirmed. Mom had Peripheral T-cell Lymphoma with a two-week survival prognosis without chemo, but at seventy-eight and in her weakened state, chemotherapy would probably kill her anyway. She reluctantly chose to fight while Dad and seven of us children stood quietly around her bed. Our sister Shirley was en route from Tennessee. Mom started chemo treatment that afternoon; however, Mom's struggle was short-lived. Within three days her blood pressure dropped dangerously low and she was transferred to ICU; five days later she died, just three weeks to the day from entering the hospital with an unknown illness.

Shocked and saddened by this tremendous loss, we clung together through our faith and sense of community within our tight-knit family, Dad, siblings, and grandchildren. We continued to gather at the farmhouse for occasional meals, fellowship, and tending to Dad's domestic needs. Dad was determined to be independent, doing laundry, dishes, cooking and cleaning, planning to survive the loss of his wife of sixty-one years. Dad silently moved forward, outwardly not displaying the sadness that affects most widowers. He traveled to Florida to our parents' winter home at Holiday Park in Lakeland, where he connected with friends. Sunny warm weather helped him endure and heal from his loss. He enjoyed the daily activities but looked forward to coming back to the farm to lend a hand to his son Hank and grandson Jamie. In mid-April, he returned, well rested and ready to plant, harvest and assist with milking his beloved dairy herd. Even at eighty-one, Dad didn't suffer from any illnesses, injuries or impairments, and was generally in good health. He didn't take pills, not even a vitamin! He continued with a routine of regular sleep, eating healthy, and staying active emotionally, physically and spiritually.

Tuesday, June 4, 2004, was a typical early summer day. Waking up that morning, we never expected a life-changing event would occur – no one ever does. I was home recuperating from a knee replacement (due to a cheerleading injury decades ago) watching the mailman deliver mail just after 1:00 p.m. As I walked down my driveway a strange, airy feeling came across my body. Looking down the road, I saw flashing in front of me one of my wildest nightmares – smoke and flames roaring from the west side of the barn, high over the top of the one hundred-sixty-foot-long structure! Without a second's hesitation, feeling my breath being sucked out of me, I hobbled back into the house and immediately called 911, giving slow, clear directions as to who I was and the location – "Barn on fire! Fully engulfed, Luchsingers on Norton Road between Young and Abbey," screaming by the time I said, "Come quickly! Barn full of cows!" I had mentally practiced the location many times for an emergency. Crossroads, address, reason. Calmly the 911 dispatcher said, "Help is on the way, thank you."

Fear, sadness, and anxiety filled my heart as I called my sister Karen at Sunset Ridge Golf course and told her simply, voice choking, "The barn is on fire, awful, it's gone, it's gone, fire out of control!" Quickly I hung up and hurried out of the house, witnessing Dad speeding by in his Dodge Dakota truck. Before I reached the end of my driveway an Onondaga County Sherriff was parking there; soon another arrived and they stayed for the remainder of the day.

Memories of my childhood, and a horrifying fear watching the devastation and destruction of our barn burning, filled my mind. It was all surreal and desperation engulfed my soul. Still struggling from the knee surgery, I walked quickly to the farm a few hundred feet away; it took all my strength. With a sense of helplessness, I stood on the lower lawn across the road in horror, watching cows and calves running from the doorway on the east side of the barn. Not until later did I realize Dad, Hank, and Jamie were unhooking the cows from their stanchions and frantically chasing the cows to

Coping With Loss

make them leave the burning barn. Dad's quick thinking and many rehearsals in his mind for any barn fire included closing all the hay holes. This bought a little more time for the cows to escape. Sadly, the family's efforts to get the cows out of the barn were fruitless – many of the cows turned around and went back into the burning barn, some from a different entrance they had left, and faced imminent death. Cows like routine and were not used to leaving the barn. They were year-round residents, a farming technique Dad learned on one of his farm tours, proven to stabilize milk production when grass in the fields was poor or summer heat affected the cows' production of milk.

    I stood alone watching helplessly as fire trucks arrived, painfully observing the out-of-control fire rising higher over the barn, swallowing up the enormous structure, and hearing the crackle of tin shearing off the gable roof, tumbling like sharp-bladed swords to the ground. From inside came the desperate bellows of suffering cows burning alive. Covering my ears, I looked up into a clear, cloudless sky to God and crying hysterically, pleaded, "Please have them die quickly! Don't let them suffer!"

    The first volunteer fireman on the scene told my father he had to leave the barn. "Dying cattle is one thing," he said, "but having to rescue people from a burning structure jeopardizes firemen's lives also." Without incident Dad left the animals he loved to the inferno and death.

Coping With Loss

One of the last pictures of the main barn before the fire

High emotions continued as volunteer fire departments from different parts of the county started to arrive, along with neighbors, friends and family. Roads were blocked off to allow firefighters and police to do their jobs, and news media stationed at the top of the hill reported live. Dark heavy smoke roaring from the fire filled the valley and could be seen for miles. The smell of burning hay and straw permeated the air.

Family members filled the front yard of the homestead and were swallowed up in disbelief at the loss of dairy cows and calves and mourned losing the beautiful barn Dad built by hand years before. We were still experiencing the loss of our mother ten months before, and now a tragic fire was too much.

Good news did exist. Some cows were still roaming around the fields surrounding the farm. They were rounded up by friends, loaded onto trucks, and transported to a new home on the Abbott farm being rented by the Cox family. Neighbors and members of the

South Onondaga Auxiliary brought in sandwiches, food, and beverages for a family grief-stricken with the death of so many animals.

Dad's brother Ed arrived and tearfully both embraced. He had his own dairy farm and knew quite well the connection farm families have with one another, and that destruction from fire causes work and dreams of a lifetime to be wiped out in one afternoon.

After the rampant blaze burned for over two hours, word spread that eight to ten cows were still alive. (It seemed impossible, for fire kills, if not by flames themselves, by inhaled smoke which takes life within minutes.) But witnesses gazing through the barn windows saw cows still alive in the northwest corner of the barn; this small corner did not go up in flames and smoke due to the northwest wind moving in the opposite direction. Concrete blocks were chiseled and cut to make a hole large enough to enter and remove the last of the herd of livestock. Dr. Mike Stack, their veterinarian, examined each animal for visual burns or injuries and one or two had to be put down. When my brother met with the insurance adjuster a day or two later, the adjuster strongly suggested none of the ten cows would survive. He was right – within a few days all the rescued cows either died or had to be put down.

Even though the hay and straw would smolder for days, the very next day clean up started. The horrific task of removing dead carcasses was urgent, and as soon as was safely possible. Decaying cattle would rapidly create an unhealthy environment. Uncle Herb

Tilden brought in his backhoe and swiftly dug a large hole, spreading across the hayfield behind the burnt-out barn, to prepare for the mass grave. Each cow had to be identified for insurance claims, and whoever could tolerate the scene recorded the number. Jamie, Hank's son had the grueling job in the burned-out basement of the barn shouting out the numbers, clipped to the ear of each cow for identifying the deceased animal, before removing her from the pit with the bucket of the backhoe. Uncle Herb then drove to the field placing the remains in the grave. He did this awful job seventy-seven times – fifty-three cows and twenty-four calves, removing and burying the lifeless animals. While recording the numbers we saw many charred cows still tied to their stanchion, eyes bulging and neck extended with feet in the gutter, trying to escape the fire. Due to severe trauma, there was evidence that several cows had partial miscarriages.

After the cows and calves were buried there was much more work to be done. Clean up was horrendous. Mike Rether, a local excavator, helped remove steel, pressing the bent, twisted and scorched sheets of metal onto a flatbed truck, separating the debris, so the wood, straw, and hay could finish burning up. The old fieldstone wall that remained next to the road was the only visual remembrance of the two-hundred-year-old foundation. Before that final wall was buried with the rest of the rubble, many family members took several stones to place in their own flower gardens as a last link to the original farm building.

There was no rebuilding, because insurance did not nearly cover what was lost in the fire. Rebuilding the dairy barn would cost a million dollars. The precious dairy farm vanished forever, along with priceless memories. Dad's guns he had owned for decades, tools he had collected over a lifetime, milking machines, a modern up-to-date bulk tank system, and an endless list of equipment necessary to run a dairy were destroyed. Most important, though, was that the fire resulted in the loss of livelihood for three families.

Change had to be made. Plan B had to be put in place. Money had to be earned for the monthly milk check would be absent. Dad was nearing eighty-two, but he still loved to work the land and had ambitious dreams. For the time being, harvesting hay, straw, wheat, and pumpkins would bring in some income. Money from the insurance was earmarked for building pole barns and possibly raising young stock. My brother was approaching sixty and tired. If anything good happened as a result of the fire, it was that he never had to get up every morning before sunrise and head to the farm for milking. His family could go to a wedding or family function without hurrying home to milk. Feeding calves and young stock did not impose a five o'clock alarm going off. Life would be easier.

Three weeks after the fire, Dad experienced persistent chest pain causing him to coil up on the couch. Volunteer fire rescue arrived and soon an ambulance. Typical signs of a heart attack were apparent. With all the stress of the fire, breathing heavy smoke, loss of his animals and livelihood, in addition to the loss of his wife ten months earlier, a heart attack was no surprise. His days of no pills or medications were over; injury to the heart dictates treatment and care. He was used to overcoming obstacles, and continued to be positive, laugh, and joke. He didn't give up because of disaster and loss – Dad believed tragedy makes us appreciate life.

After his initial hospital stay and routine recuperation at home, Dad was right back to work. He cooked for himself, including cow tongue purchased at Wal-Mart, liver and onions when eating out, Brussels sprouts, asparagus, and his well-loved limburger and head cheese. (He reminded us from time to time that head cheese is not actually cheese but tender meat from the jawbone of a pig.) Dad loved cheese even though his heart doctor encouraged him to limit eating it because of his heart condition. Swiss love cheese and Dad (one hundred percent Swiss) was no different.

The heart attack and fire did not stop him. Slowing down was not in his vocabulary. Dad loved to work just like his father. He taught us to enjoy and appreciate our work, and that happiness is what you make today, not something you hold off until the tomorrows in life. But unknown to us, our family had even more difficult struggles ahead ...

Chapter 36

Jamie

Dad taught us to tough it out. His model was to move forward, face our battles, don't fix what is not broken, and repair what needs fixing. However, with all the misfortune and hardships our family faced, Jamie's problem couldn't be fixed.

Dad's grandson Jamie and my brother Hank helped operate the farm. Each had specific jobs and responsibilities. As a teenager, Jamie played football and wrestled for Onondaga Central. A few years after high school he married Karen, and became the proud father of James Jr. and Erica. They conveniently lived just a mile from the farm. He worked seven days a week, rarely missing a day. In the winter Jamie also worked at local farms, filling in for hired men or a farmer who wanted a little time off. He was strong, healthy, dependable, and hard-working, and seldom missed an opportunity to make a little extra cash for his family.

Unfortunately, events started to change in the summer of 2006, two years after the barn fire. On occasion Jamie would come back from the field scratched, bruised, or marked up after falling. Sometimes Andrew, a neighbor, or good friend John Kelsey picked him up off the ground. When questioned about his falls, he claimed he became weak and dizzy and was unable to get up, passing off his ailment as no big deal.

    Jamie's behavior soon warranted a trip to his primary care physician. His blood sugar was over three hundred, consequently diagnosing diabetes. Even with treatment he continued to drag his leg and left side of his body. Another diagnosis of a possible stroke proved wrong. He continued to work on the farm but his responsibilities became more difficult and as months passed, there was more testing but no diagnosis could be reached even after visits to numerous specialists in Syracuse.

    The next step was a two-hour drive to Rochester, NY for further specialized testing. Several trips later Jamie's doctors in Rochester gave the family the bad news: Amyotrophic Lateral Sclerosis, ALS, sometimes called Lou Gehrig's disease. It is a rapidly progressive, invariably fatal neurological disease that affects the nerve cells in the brain and spinal cord. Knowing little about the disease the family did the heartbreaking research. Jamie, the physically powerful man we all knew, was going to experience muscle paralysis, serious limitations in swallowing and speaking and lose the ability to walk or take care of himself as the illness progressed. His hearing, seeing and touch might be the only functions he would still have as the illness advanced.

    The news devastated his wife, children, parents, sisters, brother, and enormous extended family, along with the farming

Jamie

community Jamie knew and loved. My dad and brother Hank had to face the awful fact that Jamie, the hard-working, strong guy who worked with them every day on the farm from the time he was four years old, was going to die. Despite their sorrow, they continued to act diligently as a team, focusing on picking up the slack that Jamie could no longer handle.

On April 1st, a few weeks after the sad news, Jamie celebrated his 40th birthday. The family held a surprise bittersweet birthday party with over one hundred and fifty friends, farmers and family at the Onondaga Hill Presbyterian Church Fellowship Hall.

As weeks passed researching this terrible disease, family members knew Jamie would eventually require full-time nursing care. His wife Karen needed to work and keep their medical insurance. Jamie wanted to stay home as long as he could, but his home was a raised ranch with twelve steps to the main level and just a few short months after his first symptoms he was already having difficulty climbing stairs.

In late April, Jamie's sister Wendy approached other family members suggesting a fundraiser to help with much-needed medical costs. A large amount of these costs was not covered by medical insurance. The next Sunday, cousins, aunts, sisters and close friends gathered at the same church where we had held his birthday celebration to plan. I accepted the responsibility to be chairperson and we formed committees. For seven weeks, we met every Sunday at 1:00 sharp with twenty to thirty enthusiastic friends and family and clear agenda. Each chairperson gave a brief summary about weekly accomplishments such as food donations, advertising, beverages, tickets, decorations, music, news, etc. With our diligent team players and with God's blessing, great successes were reported. Originally the event was planned for the South Onondaga Fire Department, but soon we decided it was too small. We rented a much larger facility at the New York State fairgrounds for twenty-one hundred dollars, which someone anonymously paid. Bars and taverns donated kegs of beer through a beer distribution company. Everyone knew someone who wanted to help, and we refused no one! Our team put together over fifty gift baskets valued at fifty dollars or more each. Raffles tickets were printed, flyers posted, and a boat, grill, quarter of beef, luxury recliner, golf membership at Links at Sunset Ridge, boar hunt, and a weekend get-away were a few of many donations raffled off.

Better Days Benefit for Jamie Luchsinger
A Community Comes Together

Jamie

Onondaga Central School faculty, where Jamie graduated and his children attended, donated money and gift baskets, and their PTS made over three thousand cookies. Another local golf course (Orchard Vali) volunteered to make all the food for the estimated twelve hundred people! Donated food from stores and restaurants was collected and dropped off for the cook at Orchard Vali to prepare and deliver to the fair in portable heated ovens. We planned to pay for extra food that was not donated; in the end Orchard Vali would not accept a check for the remaining expenses.

In addition to food for the luncheon, one-ounce packets of Cabot Cheese, individual bags of Terrell potato chips, and baskets of Beak and Skiff apples were arranged in decorative baskets and offered to our guests. All items were donations. Byrne Dairy donated a much-needed refrigerated truck and one thousand cartons of white and chocolate milk. Hundreds of bottles of water and cans of soda were donated from stores. Disk Jockeys and small bands offered to play music. The community had come together in a wonderful way for Jamie.

Two days before the event the *Syracuse Post Standard* ran a front-page story including a picture of Dad, my brother Hank, Jamie and his brother Bob walking across the road of the family farm with Jamie pushing a walker. The heart-wrenching story of our family's struggle with this devastating disease would touch the souls of the farm community and friends of friends who knew the Luchsingers.

On Saturday morning the local TV news media came to the

farm and interviewed the family. The fundraiser being held the next day was mentioned several times when the story was broadcast later that day. At noon on Saturday we moved everything to the fairgrounds. Donated items, gift baskets and tables were set up and decorated with green and yellow to represent John Deere, a farming icon of the Luchsinger family. Chairpersons handed out donated T-shirts to all the workers with Jamie's name and picture on them and the slogan "Fight ALS." Many pickup trucks arrived loaded with raffle items, food, beverages, and folding tables, and strong men and women to help set up. Bales of straw and farm décor decorated the entrance to the building.

Last minute preparation began at 10:30 Sunday morning with everyone's arrival, including over sixty family members and friends. Several large pizzas arrived and a few dozen donuts donated for the workers. As head chairperson I shared a word of gratitude and thanks for so many willing hands and reminded workers to eat and drink water as they might not get a chance after the benefit started at 1:00. Every chairperson delegated duties and responsibilities to their individual volunteers. We had over one hundred additional workers signed up to work different shifts, scheduled beforehand by hours on the phone.

An experienced fundraiser coordinator representing the State Fair had told our committee from the beginning we could not organize a successful fundraiser in seven weeks – impossible! But we did! And then some! He also told us to expect three to five

Jamie

hundred people at most but even before the event started we had hundreds of people lined up to pay the fifteen-dollar admission. By the time the fundraiser was over at 5:00 we had thirteen hundred paid guests. We sold beer and raffle tickets and served great food. When two raffle tables were empty my sisters and I quickly covered them to make a duplicate buffet table, serving two more buffet lines to help with the congestion of so many guests. Two first cousins, one an accountant and one a teacher, were locked in a special room and responsible for counting money (mostly cash) as it came in. They prepared a computerized spreadsheet of how much was brought in and which category the money was credited. The cash and checks collected were listed in source categories such as admission, boat raffle, boar hunt raffle, grill raffle, silent auction, and beer. Remarkably we knew the total for the day by 5:30. Eight to ten undercover police officers donated their time, neighbors and friends of Jamie's sister Kim.

    A family friend was assigned to go around to each station collecting the cash and delivering to the office every half hour throughout the afternoon. The food was great, the workers were awesome, chair people outstanding, donations tremendous, and the June weather was perfect. We had a reunion of friends and farmers from the Onondaga community, and beyond, coming out and sharing their kindness, love and generosity; so many amazing hearts. Jamie danced with his seven-year-old daughter, Erica to "Daddy's Little Girl." Tears filled our eyes. Everyone thought the same thing. He

Jamie

wouldn't be present for that special dance on her wedding day.

Over fifty thousand dollars was collected that day and taken to a night deposit with an unofficial unmarked police escort. The money went into a special account strictly for Jamie's needs.

Jamie's home had to have major renovations for his safety and comfort, with the bedroom handicap-accessible and a bathroom with special shower which was wheelchair accessible on the first floor of their raised ranch. A lift was purchased so Jamie could live on the main floor until he was confined to a wheelchair and bedridden. However, when the family approached a local contractor, Scott McClurg, to give them a quote for these renovations, Scott went back to his team of over forty employees about the circumstances. They overwhelmingly agreed to volunteer their time and expertise. Furthermore, McClurg asked subcontractors and suppliers to donate granite kitchen counters, appliances, paint, plumbing supplies etc. and the whole house received a complete makeover. The driveway was even paved. There was one condition: the family had to store their personal belongings and move out for three weeks, no peeking! They lived with Jamie's mom and dad, Hank and Eileen, during that time.

At the end of three weeks a limo company volunteered to drive Jamie and his family in a white stretch limo to the newly-renovated home. The place was beautifully decorated with modern tones of green and beige. A pink and lavender room was designed for Erica with girly accessories. James' room had baseballs and decor that an eleven-year-old boy would enjoy. Volunteer workers from McClurg's Construction attended decked out in bright blue T-shirts, along with the news media. Family members and neighbors carried purple balloons and signs. A large John Deere tractor blocked the driveway. On that early fall afternoon, the limo stopped in front as we all yelled in unison, "Move that tractor, move that tractor!" Happy smiles and cheers of joy filled our hearts. A simple reception was set up in Jamie's garage to honor and show gratitude to workers who gave up family time to help another family in need.

    We all took away a lesson about life with Jamie's struggles. Hard work individually, and as a team, can and did get the job done! We learned about love, support, compassion, and joy in the middle of turmoil, disappointment, and the inevitable sadness of Jamie's future.

Chapter 37

Hard Days

Days after the extensive renovations to Jamie's house and the excitement of moving in, reality sunk in. The family was dealing with the unknown – the medical, emotional, and financial challenges of coping with ALS. On occasion Jamie would come up to the farm, just to have a break from his "handicap environment." Jamie, a strong muscle-bound forty-year-old man, was starting to fade. Watching his grandfather and father doing work he once had done with little effort gave him desire to work again. Deep in his gut, Jamie knew this would never happen. But Jamie loved to work with a passion just like his dad and grandfather. Now he had to watch them taking up the slack for him.

Jamie was finding it more difficult each day to do routine tasks – getting out of bed, using eating utensils, and walking. His wife Karen got him up each morning, fed him scrambled eggs, helped him shower and shave, and put him in a wheelchair. She got the children ready for the bus, then left for work. Eileen, Jamie's mother, came up later in the morning to feed him lunch and watch a soap opera with him in the afternoon.

At times my brother Hank would get a call at the farm, or sometimes at home at midnight, asking him to come quickly because Jamie had fallen. In June Karen needed help to apply for Medicaid for Jamie as her medical insurance did not cover many of his bills. I gladly assisted her with the long and tedious process of completing the mounds of paperwork. Karen was exhausted with a twenty-four-hour job tending to Jamie and working outside the home.

Time after time Jamie fell and sometimes had to be taken to the hospital by ambulance with injuries. Family, neighbors and friends brought in supper. Hired nursing care from 8 a.m. to 12 p.m. to help with showering and feeding Jamie was available due to the money from the fundraiser, and this relieved some of the stress on his caregivers. As weeks and months went by he lost more strength and ability to move. A feeding tube was inserted surgically and had to be kept clean.

An Onondaga Central 1964 graduate of my class, Nancy Boston Polacek, had recently lost her husband to ALS and she was willing to sell their specialized van. Words did not have to be said as tears filled our eyes when she handed over the keys. Another 1964 classmate, Charlie Cox, paid for the van, a further heartwarming example of community camaraderie and compassion. Despite the loss of mobility and strength, ALS did not impair Jamie's mind. But verbal communication was a challenge. He had a warm and beautiful smile every day and the disease did not affect his smell, taste, or hearing. His bladder and bowel functions were normal; accidents only happened when help was unavailable or too slow to assist him to the bathroom.

As months passed Jamie had developed dysphagia, difficulty swallowing foods and liquids. At this point his food had to be the consistency of pudding. Menus were changed. His favorite foods were put in a blender. He had been receiving Meals on Wheels and they were able to deliver the special diet. Eating enough calories for him to stay healthy was a challenge; even though he was not active, his body required more food to fight to stay alive. I sewed adult bibs for him with farm related motifs – John Deere, cows, etc. His illness continued to progress and he had to be fed, but he still had that sweet smile and was grateful for any help.

Meals were planned carefully. Salmon patties were a favorite, and I prepared them frequently but all the bones had to be removed before cooking so Jamie wouldn't choke. A flavorful white sauce covered the patties with the right consistency for easy swallowing. Jamie loved salmon and that brought a smile to his face when they were delivered. Potatoes with rutabaga or carrots mashed together, tasty and nutritious was often on the menu. Fresh peas or spinach blended in the food processor were used as sides. After making several meals with ground chicken or beef, the kitchen was filled with chopping boards, kettles, frying pans and a dirty blender. Only four to six meals would be prepared at a time and some were put in the freezer. Disposable containers were used to eliminate extra work for Karen. Retired from teaching during this time, I was happy to help out.

By the summer of 2010 Jamie was in and out of the hospital with breathing problems and pneumonia. Social workers and support groups helped the family deal with the inevitable. Finally, in September Jamie was placed in Van Duyn, a nursing care facility run by the county. He would never return home. A 40-inch TV was purchased for him. He still had his mind, hearing and sight. Speech was gone and he had a feeding tube. Friends and family would visit but it was difficult to carry on a one-way conversation. A white board was placed on the wall and visitors were asked to sign in; this helped the family know who visited.

On Monday, three days before Thanksgiving, Cliff and I visited Jamie. His eyes were glassy. He had to be suctioned out three times in the short time we were there. While riding down the elevator sobbing, I looked at my husband, glanced up and said, "God, when is Jamie's suffering going to be over?"

Thanksgiving Day family members received a call that Jamie had been transferred to Upstate University Hospital. The family and medical staff decided to have the feeding tube removed and keep him comfortable. Sunday, after church, my sisters Heidi and Karen and I went to see Jamie, knowing it was saying goodbye. Heidi shaved him – he was still so handsome. God wanted us to see him peaceful, not suffering. We knew Jamie was being called home. His once strong, muscular body had given out.

The next day, November 29, 2010, Karen asked me to pick

Erica up at school, take her to the doctor, pick up a prescription, and have James and Erica over for supper as she was going to be at the hospital. After completing homework, the children were taken home to get ready for bed. Around that time the family not already there was called to the hospital. Erica and James also went. I went to stay with Dad, Jamie's sidekick on the farm. Around 9:30, Hank, Jamie's dad, called to tell us Jamie had died. Dad looked away sobbing. He didn't have to say a word. I knew what he was thinking – peace and rest at last.

Chapter 38

Change

Gone are the eighty-acre farms with fifty or sixty cows grazing in pastures. Slowly disappearing are the one-hundred-foot barns with one or two silos and electric fences surrounding the fields. Today the outward appearance of farms is larger, and new technology and modern design have shaped the farming landscape. Old hand plows sit in front yards as nostalgic mementoes, surrounded by colorful geraniums and petunias. Rustic old farm buildings with fieldstone foundations are nearly gone.

Dad's Old Hand Plow

As small farms in the community disappeared one by one, Dad became aware that macro-farming discouraged personal commitment to family and community. Large farms must run like corporations, employing herd managers, bookkeepers, and other staff, and buy on credit to keep up with technology. They have to use tax breaks and manage a large payroll with pensions, vacation time, and tenant homes.

Dad farmed with tractors unprotected from heat, cold, rain or blistering wind, and they lacked safety features. Farm tractors and equipment now have become sophisticated and high tech. Some can drive themselves and contain proper ventilation, heaters and air conditioning, radios, covered cabs with windows, wireless internet, and cell phones. GPS equipment can plow or plant fields after dark! Crops that took Dad days to harvest can now be done in an hour.

His first combine had a four-foot cut; now they have a 25-26 foot cut and cost $250,000 or more. Expensive modern equipment means less manual labor, as most farm jobs now use automated equipment. If a piece of equipment breaks down, ordering can be done on the internet from the field and delivered within hours. (Dad had to call from the house to a dealer in search of the part needed, then drive to the machinery store easily taking two or three hours from his workday.)

Weather, an important element in a farmer's day, is now forecast by computer. My dad looked at the sky or felt the air to predict the weather. He would say, "Red skies in the morning,

Change

sailors take warning; red skies at night, sailors delight." If he saw powder puff (cotton) sky it meant the earth would be dry. His favorite predictor was, "If there are sheep in the sky (cumulus clouds), no rain for forty-eight hours." Weather predictions passed down from his father were used to plan his day – plant, cut hay, bale, or do inside work. Dad was pretty good at predicting the weather!

Dad and Hank Jr. working together to collect the harvest

Dad struggled with change and the loss of the personal touch of the American farmer. The egg routes of yesteryear and farmers' self-sufficiency have vanished. Corporate chain stores have replaced the struggling middle-class owners of feed, machinery, and hardware stores that used to serve suburban communities. Many small intimate churches have combined with others churches to form a large congregation. Local grocery stores have been replaced with modern big box stores and specialty shops in malls with post-modern designs. Farmland has been sold to construct beautiful golf courses in country settings.

Change

But with advancement in technology, supermarket consumerism, the changing role of farmers, financial investments, and urbanites moving to the country, the new corporate farmer has new problems. Farmers have to be conscious of the consumer, and know their needs and wants. Consumer desires created by smart advertising have orchestrated people's ways of thinking about what they purchase and eat. As needs of urban communities change, so does supply and demand. The dairy business has suffered because some people believe there are healthier alternatives than, "Milk is the perfect food." (This slogan I taught our four sons as they guzzled down seven to ten gallons of milk each week.) Fluid milk is not a regular part of some diets because the corporations have told the consumer that milk and dairy products have too much fat and there are better choices for good health. Expensive juice boxes, soda, bottled juices and flavored water have replaced milk at the dinner table, all cheaper to produce and therefore generating a larger profit. Powdered substitutes to make frozen shakes are now usually served at fast food restaurants and the good homemade custard cones are gone, replaced with powdered ingredients. (At Pfeiffer's Drive In, I made milkshakes using only milk, ice cream, and two squirts of flavoring.) Health reports and news media still often maintain that butter, ice cream, and cheese should be limited in our diets due to too much fat. New studies suggest eating butter, drinking milk, and using real dairy products aren't bad for us if eaten in moderation. (I have learned moderation is the key to almost everything in my seventy-plus years of life's lessons.) Dad drank milk every day, rich Jersey milk and lots of it, and lived a very long time!

Rural landscapes have changed drastically – old buildings torn down or bulldozed over, and large one-story pole barns constructed in their place. Dad was astonished but also overwhelmed with this transformation. He liked to keep things the same and thought technology was moving too quickly. But "new farmers" are faced with their own challenges. Keeping current is a struggle with the changing laws that dictate proper drainage, soil conservation, strip farming, and expensive irrigation systems which consequently create phenomenal costs to farmers. Farmers must now produce large quantities of feed for their animals and milk hundreds of cows to economically make ends meet. They have to own or rent hundreds of acres of tillable land, be willing to take risks, and have good credit to borrow tens of thousands of dollars at a time to readily expand, purchase necessary equipment, and build new buildings to keep their farms afloat.

Baling hay, pulling a bale off the wagon one at a time, physically picking stone from the fields in early spring, or the backbreaking job of shoveling manure into wheelbarrows from the gutters and wheeling it up a two-by-ten-inch plank to dump into the manure spreader were tough jobs of the past. This intense work took a physical toll on the body. Computer-generated equipment feeds livestock and cell phones and GPS improve management techniques. Four-wheelers cut down on tiresome walking from field to field or

Change

barn to barn and forklifts and bobcats eliminate physically lifting stones or moving a stump from a field. Tractors have special lifts to move bales of hay weighing several hundred pounds (wrapped in white plastic and looking like giant marshmallows or dinosaur eggs) that are stored by the sides of the newly-made pole barns, replacing the hayloft of decades ago. Automatic barn cleaners and milking parlors have made the painful physical part of farming less demanding.

    But with change comes other troubles and concerns. Farmers have to accept the urban America that has settled into farming communities. Onondaga Community College is located four miles from our family farm, and Syracuse city limits just six miles, and so water, gas, and sewer demands are increased by the newest members of rural living. With a little campaigning, the new owners vote in expensive water, gas, and sewer systems that are installed along country roads. These cost hundreds of dollars each year, for twenty or thirty years, in the form of taxes. Many new residents dislike early morning farm activity, the smell of cow manure, electric fences and slow-moving equipment on the roads, all of which create disquietude for new residents who don't quite understand the reality of managing dairy farms.

    Our society is on the move – we can get lunch from a vending machine or buy hot coffee in the morning at the drive-thru (if you are willing to take five minutes to wait in line with ten cars in front of you!) Technology and inexpensive supermarket consumerism encourage canned and frozen fruits and vegetables, so farm wives feel it's a waste of precious time and energy to buy seeds, plant, weed, harvest, and process them in a hot kitchen when they can be purchased what they need for dollar or two. Families are leaving this skill to the Amish or novelty stores using brilliant marketing techniques to sell jams, vegetables, fruits, or specialty pickles for four or five dollars a jar, reminiscent of bygone days. I still attempt the tiring task of canning tomatoes, making Grandma Tilden's chili sauce, peaches, or bread and butter pickles occasionally, but it's not economical unless the produce comes from my garden or someone has extra to give me.

Farm children have their own dreams and find it difficult to commit to the immense work of a farm. They expect a decent wage (a salary our culture demands) along with medical coverage, pensions, and benefits. Too many high cost risks in farming, and better job opportunities elsewhere, along with pressure from urban society, affected us. Continuously influenced by urban culture – malls, designer clothes, movies, cars, Facebook, cell phones, and their friends, farm children have the same materialistic wants of youth in towns or suburban America. A few children stay, others find interest in other occupations. One good thing – most farm children, because of their strict up-bringing, know how to work and are dependable and desirable employees.

Farming has always been the heart of America, but Dad in time couldn't compete. Now hired help allows farmers to take family vacations and farmers own computers that assist in all aspects of farming. Farm equipment is purchased new, instead of the "repair, recycle, or fix what is broken" approach my Dad had. Dad's way of surviving was supplementing his income, seeking out ways to earn cash, as most farmers did during his era. For generations, a pattern of shared attitudes, ideas and goals have united farmers across our country. Most farmers now have a better standard of living than my Dad's generation but he did survive on his own terms.

Chapter 39

One Final Thought

On the farm we saw animals being born and animals dying. That was life on the farm. It reminds us that our own lives are filled with arrivals and departures. Dad died at home on March 7, 2016 at 93. On his 92nd birthday, his silver hair blew in the wind as he drove his John Deere tractor, hauling a load of freshly-baled hay past my home, the home he helped build.

Dad was smart, even though his formal education ended in eighth grade – he fixed equipment, committed to memory important details, a talented carpenter, loved his work, and passionate about the farm. Our father always had valued advice, and a role model to us eight kids. He knew many four-letter words but the one that meant the most to him was WORK. My father was taught the value of hard work from his father, the penniless immigrant from Switzerland. Dad shared many stories about his childhood and early marriage: milking twenty-five cows by hand, handling a team of stubborn workhorses, remodeling kitchens, building homes, working an eight-hour a day job away from the farm five days a week, picking up potatoes for three cents a bushel – jobs most of us only read about.

He never complained about long hours working in physically challenging jobs.

On rainy or snowy days Dad repaired or sharpened tools and equipment to get a jump on the busy summer season. You could find him in the shed fixing or welding. He might squeeze in a short power nap in the afternoon. Sometimes those rainy days were used to visit with a neighbor, or for a much needed rest, a welcomed gift from God.

Farm equipment cost money, lots of it. He greased machines and kept tools clean and maintained. This attitude was instilled in me, to take care of my belongings and treat them with respect. Dad fixed or repaired his equipment or tools before he bought anything new.

Dad had epic struggles but dealt with conflicts. He experienced the unexpected deaths of prized cows, injuries and illness, the death of his wife of sixty-one years after a brief illness, and his adult grandson with ALS, a pillar on the farm. Dad persevered after the horrific fire of the family farm which destroyed barns he built by hand from timber logged from his own woods along with his beloved dairy cows. A lifetime of work vanished in one afternoon! But during these tragedies and hardships Dad grieved appropriately and moved forward.

I have the deepest gratitude to a father who shaped my character. Throughout my life he taught me simple lessons. My father was attentive and focused on his work, staying between the

One Final Thought

rows when he planted his crops; we knew if we strayed outside the lines in our lives we would needlessly destroy them. Dad taught us not to damage anything we nurtured, including family, friends, and our jobs. He took time to hug a child, or give special attention to one of his twenty-two grandchildren, thirty-nine great-grandchildren, or a neighbor kid.

2007 – Dad with my grandson Alex

Dad died rich, not in money, but with a huge family, many friends, and neighbors who respected his teachings. He was an amazing man!

One Final Thought

Family Recipes

During the 1950's and '60's kitchen tools, small appliances, and equipment to cook with were limited. We prepared our food using double boilers, meat cleavers, percolators, and cast iron frying pans. We had no microwaves, meat thermometers, food choppers or food processors (except the wooden bowl we used to chop cabbage, onions, and green peppers), no blenders, K-cup coffee pots, toaster ovens or crock pots. Our meals were prepared from food raised or grown on the farm; eggs, milk, beef, chicken, pork, preserved garden produce, potatoes, lard, wild game and basic staples including flour, sugar, and oatmeal. Cooking and preparing food took much longer but was done lovingly with perfect results.

The instructions for some of the family recipes are prepared using a cast iron frying pan or double boiler. You may prepare these recipes using modern kitchen tools with the same results, as long as you include the love.

Grandma Tilden's Chocolate Cookies

¼ cup butter
¼ cup shortening
1 cup sugar
1 egg
½ cup sour milk*

1 tsp. baking soda
½ tsp. salt
2 cups flour
1 tsp. vanilla
1/3 cup baking cocoa

*To make sour milk, add two tablespoons of vinegar to milk, and set aside for one hour.

Cream together butter, shortening, sugar, and egg. Add dry ingredients to creamed mixture, then add milk and vanilla mixing well. Drop tablespoons of batter on to greased cookie sheet. Bake for 10 - 12 minutes at 350 F. Makes about 30 cookies. Frost if you like.

Grandma made these cookies once a week while babysitting and cleaning for Mom while she worked. We have fond memories of coming home from school and finding these cookies in the round Tupperware container. Two or three cookies and a glass of ice cold milk was savored by all – and kept us content until our 6:30 supper.

German Green Beans

1 lb. cut green beans	¼ cup sugar
2 rounded Tbsp. flour	½ onion – diced
salt and pepper	¼ cup cider vinegar
1 cup water	
¼ lb. bacon sliced in small pieces	

You may use fresh, frozen or canned beans. Cook beans first if they are fresh or frozen saving water to add to other ingredients. Sauté bacon and onion together in cast iron frying pan on medium heat until tender, but do not drain fat. Sprinkle flour over bacon mixture and slowly add one cup of water, stirring, add sugar and vinegar allowing this to thicken to form gravy. Add cooked beans with the (little) water left in cooking pot; add salt and pepper. Simmer for several minutes. Add more water if too thick. Makes four servings.

Dad liked this side dish because of the sweet and sour flavor. We usually had all the ingredients on hand and quick and easy to prepare. It was served often, especially during winter months. Use more or less bacon and onion as desired. I use one teaspoon celery seed in my dish but we didn't have it available as a kid.

Family Recipes

Boiled Raisin Cookies

1 cup raisins	½ tsp. vanilla
½ cup water	½ tsp. baking powder
1 cup sugar	¼ tsp. allspice
½ cup shortening	½ tsp. salt
2 eggs	¾ tsp. cinnamon
2 cups flour	¼ tsp. nutmeg
½ tsp. soda	

Boil 1 cup raisins in ½ cup of water for 5 minutes. Cool to room temperature (do not drain). Cream sugar and shortening. Add eggs, mixing well. Sift together flour, soda, baking powder, salt, cinnamon, nutmeg, allspice. Add one half of flour mixture to batter. Add raisins and remaining flour mixture and vanilla, mixing well. Bake at 375 F. for 10-12 minutes on greased cookie sheet. Makes 4 dozen.

Mom made a double batch at a time. They were still delicious one or two days later, but usually never lasted that long. She bought raisins when she planned on making these cookies. Dad loved anything that had raisins in them!

Family Recipes

Barbecued Chicken Sauce

For 10 Halves

1 qt. cider vinegar	2/3 cup salt
1 ½ cups salad oil	2 Tbsp. poultry seasoning
2 tsp. black pepper	1 raw egg

Beat above ingredients together. Baste chicken with sauce every five minutes after turning until done (about one hour depending on size of pieces and temperature of grill).

Dad was given this recipe from his brother Pete who was involved in an annual Boy Scout barbeque chicken fundraiser in the 1950's. He said it was the "Cornell recipe." Growing up, this recipe was used every Sunday during the summer months barbecuing freshly killed chickens cooked on a wood fire Dad made with perfection. With new health warning about too much salt, I reluctantly use about half the amount (1/3 cup) and also marinate the chicken overnight in the refrigerator.

Mom's Date Nut Cake

1 cup sugar	1 tsp. baking powder
1 Tbsp. butter	1 tsp. salt
1 egg	1 tsp. vanilla
1 cup dates	1 cup nuts
1 ½ cups flour	

Cut dates into pieces, pour 1 cup hot water over dates and stir in 1 tsp. baking soda. Let cool. Combine sugar, butter, and egg, mixing well. Add flour, baking powder, salt and vanilla to sugar, butter, and egg mixture stirring well. Add nuts and date mixture to batter. (Batter will be thin.) Pour into greased 9 X 9" pan. Bake at 350 F. for 45 minutes.

Mom made this yummy homemade cake for company or holiday time. Dad liked it plain but sometimes Mom sent one of us kids to the milk house with a plastic container to skim cream off the top of the can of milk in the cooler. We didn't do it too often because butterfat from Jersey cows was important and gave us a bigger milk check. Date Nut Cake with real whipped cream was the best!!

Fried Squash

3-4 small summer squash   ½ stick butter
1 medium onion   salt and pepper

Using our handy cast iron frying pan, melt butter, add thinly sliced yellow summer squash and onion. Salt and pepper to taste. Fry squash on medium temperature, turning it every minute or two until tender. Cover in between turning. Watch for burning!

Easy, quick, and one of Dad's favorites! When the summer squash was young and tender, we prepared this easy dish several times a week. Dad loved vegetables and ate a hardy helping every time!

Vanilla Cream Graham Cracker Pie

Graham Cracker Shell

1 ¼ cups graham crackers (crushed) - about 1 package

1/3 cup sugar

5 Tbsp. butter

Preheat oven to 375 F. Melt butter in microwave using 8 or 9" glass pie tin (30 seconds). Add crumbs, sugar to melted butter, mixing well; save 1/3 cup crumbs for top! Form remaining crumb mixture around edges and bottom of pie dish. Bake in oven for 8-9 minutes until lightly brown around edges.

Vanilla Pudding

¾ cup sugar	2 cups whole milk
1/3 cup flour	2 Tbsp. butter
½ tsp. salt	2 tsp. vanilla
3 egg yolks-beaten (save whites)	

Measure milk into microwave-safe four-cup bowl (or larger). Add sugar, flour and salt and mix. Add beaten egg yolks, mixing well with a whisk. Microwave for two minutes, remove, whisk, return to microwave, one more minute, repeat one or two more times until mixture has thickened. Stir in vanilla and butter. Pour into baked graham cracker pie shell.

Family Recipes

Meringue

Beat egg whites using electric mixer, add two tablespoons sugar and beat until fluffy. Dollop on top of pie filling, spreading meringue around gently. Sprinkle the graham cracker mixture that was set aside on top. Bake at 375 F for about 12 minutes until the meringues lightly brown on top.

The best! For our Sunday dinners we made a double recipe using our 12-inch pie dish. Each one of us took a turn cleaning the pie dish each week. Mom used a double boiler when making her filling and separated the eggs adding at the end. She melted the butter in the oven. Now with the convenience of a microwave several steps have been eliminated and the preparation time is cut in half. We used our own eggs, milk, and butter.

Hamburg Gravy

1 pound hamburger   1 small onion finely chopped
1 cup water   2 Tbsp. Worcestershire sauce
1 cup milk   salt & pepper
3 Tbsp. flour

In a large frying pan, sauté onions with hamburger until onions are tender and pink color is gone from the beef. Sprinkle flour over meat blending well. Slowly add water and milk stirring as it thickens. Add Worcestershire sauce and salt and pepper. Let it simmer for five minutes. It is done! The recipe will serve four hardy appetites.

Dad loved mashed potatoes and this easy, quick dish was an old standby at mealtime. We doubled the above recipe. Our ground meat was packaged in two-pound packages before being placed in the freezer so a good amount was made. We peeled a kettle of potatoes and after mashing added lots of butter and milk.

Swiss Steak

2- 3 lbs. round steak	½ cup flour
2 – 3 Tbsp. shortening	salt & pepper
1 medium onion	2 Tbsp. Worcestershire sauce
1 quart tomatoes	½ green pepper (optional)

Cut round steak into serving-size pieces, pound out using mallet to tenderize. In pie plate add flour, salt and pepper, mixing. Add pieces of meat covering all sides.

In large cast iron frying pan, melt shortening; add meat browning on each side. Remove meat. Add thinly sliced onion, browning (3 or 4 minutes) adding more shortening if needed. Add meat back into pan, tomatoes, 1 cup of water, Worcestershire sauce, mix and cover, simmering on low heat for one-half hour.

Remove meat; thicken broth if needed with 2 tablespoons flour and ½ cup of water. Add more salt and pepper if desired. Return meat to gravy and serve with real mashed potatoes or noodles. Excellent the next day. Serves 6 – 8.

After browning, you can use a crock pot or slow cooker with the same results. Remember always use your toughest cut of meat – comes out delicious, tender, and flavorsome.

Family Recipes

Dad loved Swiss steak along with buttery mashed potatoes! Stored for winter were canned tomatoes, onions, and potatoes from the garden. So when Mom brought up a package of round steak from the freezer, we knew Swiss steak was on the menu. We never had leftovers! In fact we never had ANY leftovers at any meal! Sometimes Mom made Swiss steak using venison, but I always knew.

Oyster Stew

½ cup butter

1 quart whole milk

1 pound container of fresh oysters (do not drain)

salt and pepper to taste

Melt butter with milk. Add oysters and liquid. Heat up but do not boil (watch it!) Stew is ready when oysters curl at their ends.

Oyster stew was traditionally served Christmas Eve at our house. Seafood was popular during the Christmas season at the supermarket and it was a splurge. Dad used to have oyster stew as kid served Christmas Eve and Mom wanted to carry through as a special treat for him.

Apple Cake with Vanilla Sauce

4-5 apples   2 tsp. cinnamon
½ cup sugar

Peel apples, slice thin, mix sugar and cinnamon into apples and place in bottom of a greased 9 by 13" pan. Set aside. Make batter.

Cake Batter

1 1/4 cups sugar   2 cups flour
½ cup shortening   3 tsp. baking powder
3 eggs   1 tsp. salt
1 cup milk   1 tsp. vanilla

Cream together shortening and sugar, then add eggs, beating. Mix together flour, baking powder and salt and add alternately with milk to the creamed mixture. Blend well, add vanilla. Pour evenly over prepared apple mixture. Bake at 350 F for 45 minutes or until cake springs back when touched.

Vanilla Sauce

½ cup brown sugar   2 Tbsp. butter
1 Tbsp. flour   1 ¼ cups whole milk
¼ tsp. cinnamon   pinch of salt
1 egg - beaten   1 Tbsp. vanilla

Family Recipes

Melt butter on stove in heavy saucepan. Add sugar, flour, and cinnamon, beaten egg, milk, and salt to melted butter, whisking well together. Heat over medium heat stirring until thickened - about 10 minutes Add vanilla and serve warm. Mom used to use a double boiler – it prevented scorching.

* Much easier using a microwave. After adding ingredients, cook in microwave stopping every minute to stir until it is the desired consistency.

Mom made this luscious dessert during the apple season, using ingredients and staples we had on hand. Sounds like a lot of steps, but really only takes a few minutes to prepare and well worth the effort.

Best Lemon Meringue Pie – Microwave

1 - 9 inch pie shell baked	3 egg yolks
2 cups warm water	½ cup pure lemon juice
1 ½ cups sugar (scant)	1 tsp. lemon rind (opt.)
¼ cup cornstarch	3 Tbsp. butter (opt.)
3 Tbsp. flour	

Separate eggs; Save egg whites for meringue, set aside. Use a large glass microwave bowl (I use an 8 cup measuring pitcher with handle.) Add each ingredient to water whisking after each addition. Microwave three minutes. Take out and stir. Repeat until filling has started to thicken. It will be consistency of pudding. Pour into baked pie shell. Prepare Meringue by beating egg whites and 2 T of sugar with electric mixer until soft peaks appear. Spread meringue completely over pie filling sealing edges. Bake 10-12 minutes.

I make this recipe often at Holiday Park in Florida, serve to my northern visitors, take it to pot luck and street block parties, and enjoy watching the pie disappear. My mother told me Great-Grandma Tilden made a delicious homemade lemon meringue pie before microwaves and bottled lemon juice. It took her all morning to make.

Sloppy Joe

1 lb. ground beef	1 Tbsp. Worcestershire sauce
½ cup chopped onion	3 Tbsp. vinegar
½ cup chopped celery	2 Tbsp. sugar
1 tsp. mustard	½ cup ketchup
½ cup water	black pepper to taste
1 8 oz. can tomato sauce	

Sauté onion and celery with one tablespoon shortening until tender. Add ground beef and brown slowly. Add remaining ingredients and mix well. Simmer for 20 – 30 minutes stirring occasionally. Serve on hamburger buns. Makes 4 servings. If you like it sweeter, add another tablespoon of sugar.

This recipe is similar to the Sloppy Joe served in the 60's for lunch at school. When my four children were growing up and with my busy life, I made a large batch and froze into meal-size servings adding a salad and fruit cup – dinner was ready!

A Final Note from the Author

Life is full of obstacles. Sickness, family emergencies, celebrations, and death of loved ones often get in the way of realizing our dreams. It took me eight years to complete this book, but I was determined. I learned from my dad to have a vision, stay focused, and never give up. I hope you take something from this book, from the life stories of my family, which have a common theme of perseverance, struggles, community, and love. I am thankful I was given the opportunity to spend many hours with my dad during good times and through his illness, learning about his life's story.

2000 – Dad's Farm

Made in the USA
Columbia, SC
23 October 2017